11+ Verbal Reasoning

For **GL** Assessment

Benchmark Test

This book contains two pull-out sections:

A **Benchmark Test** at the front
A **Parents' Guide to 11+ Verbal Reasoning** at the back

Study Book
and Parents' Guide

Section Three

Find the letter that will finish the first word and start the second word of each pair.
The same letter must be used for both pairs.

1. her (?) we   und (?) at   (____)
2. lo (?) est   ste (?) arm   (____)
3. spi (?) ail   wi (?) ew   (____)
4. ra (?) ap   fi (?) ift   (____)
5. po (?) eep   sa (?) ame   (____)   / 5

Underline two words, one from each set of brackets, that complete the sentence in the best way.

6. **Ground** is to (earth walk below) as **sky** is to (bird above cloud).
7. **Right** is to (left correct due) as **wrong** is to (bad fail mistaken).
8. **Clock** is to (tick minute time) as **compass** is to (walker needle direction).
9. **Play** is to (happy fun game) as **cook** is to (food kitchen chef).
10. **Smile** is to (mouth grin face) as **sneeze** is to (unwell tissue nose).   / 5

Find the number that continues each sequence in the best way. Write your answer on the line.

11. **25**   20   16   13   11   (____)
12. **5**   8   6   9   7   (____)
13. **14**   13   13   14   16   (____)
14. **96**   48   24   12   6   (____)
15. **4**   9   16   25   36   (____)   / 5

The number codes for three of these four words are listed in a random order.
Work out the code to answer the questions.

FOOL   ALSO   FLAW   LOWS

5132   4156   4221

16. Find the code for the word **LOWS**.   (_____)
17. Find the code for the word **SOLO**.   (_____)
18. Find the word that has the number code **4251**. (_____)
19. Find the word that has the number code **4126**. (_____)   / 4

Read the information carefully, then use it to answer the question that follows.

20. George, Zara, Norman, Cindy and Hamit all collect badges.
    Hamit has more badges than Cindy. Norman has half as many badges as Hamit.
    George has more badges than Hamit. Zara has more badges than George.

    If these statements are true, only one of the sentences below **must** be true. Which one?

    A Norman has more badges than Hamit.
    B George has fewer badges than Cindy.
    C Cindy has fewer badges than Norman.
    D Zara has the most badges.
    E George has the fewest badges.   / 1

END OF TEST   / 20

Section Two

Find the word that completes the third pair of words so that it follows the same pattern as the first two pairs. Write your answer on the line.

1. treat eat   spill ill   frown (_____)
2. plead pea   bound bun   whine (_____)
3. prime rip   gleam leg   trams (_____)
4. whole low   grabs bag   trunk (_____)

/ 4

Underline the word that has the most opposite meaning to the word in capital letters.

5. **CURLY**   wavy   straight   uneven   hard
6. **LOOSEN**   slacken   wobbly   adjust   squeeze
7. **FEW**   many   solo   seldom   enough
8. **COWARDLY**   hero   unhappy   brave   flee
9. **JOLLY**   funny   boring   sad   hungry

/ 5

Each letter stands for a number. Work out the answer to each sum as a letter. Write your answer on the line.

10. A = 3 B = 4 C = 5 D = 7 E = 10   D − B = (____)
11. A = 5 B = 6 C = 10 D = 15 E = 16   B + C = (____)
12. A = 3 B = 4 C = 9 D = 12 E = 13   D ÷ A = (____)
13. A = 2 B = 6 C = 8 D = 10 E = 14   D + A − B = (____)
14. A = 2 B = 5 C = 7 D = 15 E = 17   A × B + B = (____)

/ 5

Find the pair of letters that completes each sentence in the most sensible way. Use the alphabet to help you: A B C D E F G H I J K L M N O P Q R S T U V W X Y Z

15. **HN** is to **JP** as **QT** is to (____).
16. **AV** is to **XS** as **ES** is to (____).
17. **UM** is to **WL** as **LR** is to (____).
18. **GP** is to **DR** as **KD** is to (____).

/ 4

Read the information carefully, then use it to answer the question that follows. Write your answer on the line.

19. Susie, Rachael, Gareth, Stuart and Abdul are discussing the types of books they like.

    Susie and Gareth like autobiographies and science fiction. Stuart and Abdul like true crime. Everyone but Gareth likes historical books. Rachael likes romance novels.

    Who likes the **most** types of book?   (_____)

20. Jenny, Ivan, Pascal, Oscar and Steve are discussing their favourite fast food.

    Everyone except Oscar likes burgers. Ivan, Jenny and Steve all like chips. Oscar and Pascal like chicken nuggets. Ivan and Steve like pizza.

    Who likes the **fewest** types of fast food?   (_____)

/ 2

/ 20

11+ Verbal Reasoning — Benchmark Test

There are 60 questions in this test and it should take about 40 minutes. Fill in your answer according to the question instructions. If you get stuck on a question, move on to the next one.

Section One

In each sentence below a three-letter word is hidden at the end of one word and the start of the next. Underline the part of the sentence that contains the hidden word and write the word on the line.

1. She stood delicately. (_____)
2. We bought some sandwiches. (_____)
3. She had a calico gown. (_____)
4. Ogres are smelly and ugly. (_____)
5. Bring other shoes tomorrow. (_____)

/ 5

Three of the words in each list are linked. Underline the word that is **not** related to the other three.

6. mountain   cliff   hill   field
7. stone   water   pebble   rock
8. zebra   giraffe   hippo   dog
9. beef   ham   potato   bacon
10. December   August   July   June

/ 5

Find the missing number to complete each sum. Write your answer on the line.

11. 3 × 5 = (____)
12. 9 ÷ 3 = 1 + (____)
13. 8 − 6 = 4 ÷ (____)
14. 5 + 9 = 10 + (____)

/ 4

Each question uses a different code. Use the alphabet to help you work out the answer to each question: A B C D E F G H I J K L M N O P Q R S T U V W X Y Z

15. If the code for **SIX** is **UKZ**, what is **RKI** the code for? (_____)
16. If the code for **SKY** is **PHV**, what is the code for **WAG**? (_____)
17. If the code for **PIP** is **LKL**, what is the code for **ZOO**? (_____)
18. If the code for **PUG** is **SUJ**, what is **ZIJ** the code for? (_____)

/ 4

Read the statements below, then circle the sentence (A-C) that **must** be true.

19. Crows are a type of bird. Birds have feathers.
    A Crows are black.   **B** All birds are crows.   **C** Crows have feathers.
20. Sam is a vet. Vets treat sick animals.
    A Sam treats sick animals.   **B** Sam is a man.   **C** All animals are sick.

/ 2

/ 20

© CGP 2019

VHRE2

11+ Verbal Reasoning

For GL Assessment

Preparing for the 11+ is a tricky business, but never fear — CGP is here to explain everything children (and parents) need to know about Verbal Reasoning!

We've packed this fantastic book with crystal-clear study notes, tips and examples, plus plenty of practice questions to put their skills to the test.

We've also included a helpful pull-out Parents' Guide, along with a Benchmark Test that's perfect for spotting children's strengths — and any areas they need to improve.

How to access your free Online Edition

This book includes a free Online Edition to read on your PC, Mac or tablet. You'll just need to go to **cgpbooks.co.uk/extras** and enter this code:

1346 9266 3495 2799

By the way, this code only works for one person. If somebody else has used this book before you, they might have already claimed the Online Edition.

Study Book
and Parents' Guide

Contents

About the 11+

What's in the 11+ 1
What's in the 11+ Verbal Reasoning Test 2
How to Prepare for the 11+ 3

Section One — The Alphabet

Tick off the check box for each topic as you go along.

Alphabet Positions .... 4 ✓
Identify a Letter From a Clue 6
Alphabetical Order 8

Section Two — Making Words

Preparing for the Test 10
Missing Letters 12
Move a Letter 14
Hidden Word 16
Find the Missing Word 18
Use a Rule to Make a Word 20
Compound Words 22
Complete a Word Pair 24
Anagram in a Sentence 26
Word Ladders 28

Section Three — Word Meanings

Preparing for the Test 29
Closest Meaning 31
Opposite Meaning 34
Multiple Meanings 37
Odd Ones Out 40
Word Connections 42
Reorder Words to Make a Sentence 45

Section Four — Maths and Sequences

Preparing for the Test... 47
Complete the Sum 49
Letter Sequences... 51
Number Sequences... 54
Related Numbers 57
Letter-Coded Sums.. 60

Section Five — Logic and Coding

Preparing for the Test... 62
Letter Connections 63
Letter-Word Codes 65
Number-Word Codes 68
Explore the Facts 70
Solve the Riddle.. 72
Word Grids 75

Glossary... 77
Answers... 78
Index 84

Published by CGP

Editors:
Claire Boulter, Heather Gregson, Holly Poynton, Jo Sharrock

With thanks to Joe Brazier and Samantha Bensted for the proofreading.

With thanks to the moderators of ElevenPlusExams.co.uk for their input.

ISBN: 978 1 78908 178 7

Printed by Elanders Ltd, Newcastle upon Tyne.
Clipart from Corel®

Based on the classic CGP style created by Richard Parsons.

Text, design, layout and original illustrations © Coordination Group Publications Ltd. (CGP) 2019
All rights reserved.

Photocopying more than one section of this book is not permitted, even if you have a CLA licence.
Extra copies are available from CGP with next day delivery • 0800 1712 712 • www.cgpbooks.co.uk

About the 11+

What's in the 11+

Here's a quick overview of what's in the 11+ to help you get your head round the basics.

The 11+ is an Admissions Test

1) The 11+ is a test used by some schools to help with their selection process.
2) You'll usually take it when you're in Year 6, at some point during the autumn term.
3) Schools use the results to decide who to accept. They might also use other things to help make up their mind, like information about where you live.

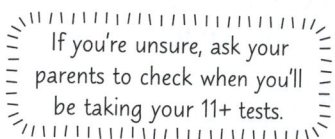
If you're unsure, ask your parents to check when you'll be taking your 11+ tests.

Some Schools test a Mixture of Subjects

1) There are four main subjects that can be tested in the 11+, so depending on the school you're applying for, you might sit papers on some or all of these:

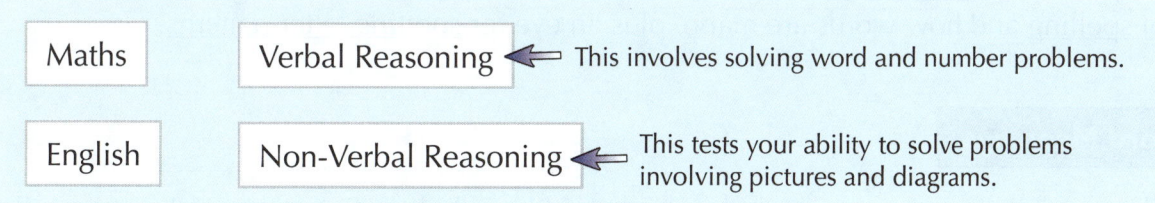

- Maths
- English
- Verbal Reasoning ← This involves solving word and number problems.
- Non-Verbal Reasoning ← This tests your ability to solve problems involving pictures and diagrams.

2) This book will help you with the Verbal Reasoning part of the test.

Get to Know what Kind of Paper you're taking

Your paper will either be multiple choice or standard answer.

Multiple Choice

1) For each question you'll be given some options on a separate answer sheet.
2) You'll need to mark your answer with a clear pencil line in the box next to the option that you think is correct.

Look out for the 'Tips and Tricks' boxes in this Study Book — they'll give you practical advice about the test.

Standard Answer

1) You'll have to write down the correct answer for some questions, but you may have some options to choose from for others.
2) You'll usually mark or write your answer on the question paper.

Check which type of question paper you'll be taking, so you know what it looks like and where your answers go. Try to do some practice tests in the same format as the test you'll be taking, so you know what to expect on the day.

What's in the 11+ Verbal Reasoning Test

Get your brain ready for Verbal Reasoning by reading about the different question types.

Verbal Reasoning involves Solving Problems

1) Although you won't have learnt how to answer Verbal Reasoning questions at school, you've probably already picked up some of the skills you need for the test.
2) There are lots of different question types that can crop up. We've grouped them into categories:

The Alphabet

You'll need to use the alphabet to answer these questions. Knowing your alphabet inside out will really help you.

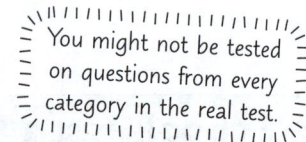
You might not be tested on questions from every category in the real test.

Making Words

You'll need to form words using other words or letters. You'll need a good grasp of spelling and how words are made, plus an eye for spotting letter patterns.

Word Meanings

These questions test your vocabulary and word knowledge. Questions of this type will ask you to think about the meanings of words or find connections between them.

Maths and Sequences

You'll need to show that you can work with numbers. Make sure your mental maths is up to scratch, as well as your times tables and basic maths skills. For sequence questions, you'll need to spot letter or number patterns and find the next step.

Logic and Coding

For logic questions, you'll need to show that you understand information and can pick out the key points. Coding questions will test your maths and logic skills, as well as your ability to spot rules and complete patterns.

3) Certain question types in these categories come up more often than others in the test.
4) We've labelled these questions as 'Key Questions' in this Study Book to show you which are the most important question types.
5) This doesn't mean you should ignore the rest — it's just to show you which questions to focus on, especially if you're pushed for time.

This book includes several different methods for solving the common question types. Try using different methods to see which ones work best for you.

About the 11+

How to Prepare for the 11+

Give yourself a head start with your Verbal Reasoning preparation — be organised and plan ahead.

Divide your Preparation into Stages

1) You should find a way to prepare for the 11+ that suits you. This may depend on how much time you have before the test. Here's a good way to plan your Verbal Reasoning practice:

> Do the Benchmark Test at the front of this book. Ask an adult to mark it for you.
>
> ↓
>
> Learn strategies for answering different question types using this Study Book. Use the smiley face tick boxes at the end of each topic to record how confident you feel about tackling different question types.
>
> ↓
>
> Do plenty of practice questions, concentrating on the question types you find tricky.
>
> ↓
>
> Sit some practice papers to prepare you for the real test.

2) When you first start answering Verbal Reasoning questions, try to solve the questions without making any mistakes, rather than working quickly.
3) Once you feel confident about the questions, then you can build up your speed.
4) You can do this by asking an adult to time you as you answer a set of questions, or by seeing how many questions you can answer in a certain amount of time, e.g. 5 minutes. You can then try to beat your time or score.
5) As you get closer to the test day, work on getting a balance between speed and accuracy — that's what you're aiming for when you sit the real test.

There are Many Ways to Practise the Skills you Need

The best way to tackle Verbal Reasoning is to do lots of practice. This isn't the only thing that will help though — there are other ways you can build up the skills you need for the test:

1) Read a mix of fiction and non-fiction — poetry, newspapers, novels etc.
2) If you come across any unfamiliar words, look them up in a dictionary. Keeping a vocabulary list is a great way to remember new words.
3) Play word games or do crosswords to build up your vocabulary.
4) Practise your times tables with a friend by taking it in turns to test each other.
5) Play games like 'Twenty Questions' or 'Cluedo' to help you think logically and draw conclusions based on information that you're given.

Section One — The Alphabet

Alphabet Positions

These pages will make questions on the alphabet as easy as A, B, C...

Warm-Up Activity

Use the code below to match these numbers to letters and work out the punch line to the joke.

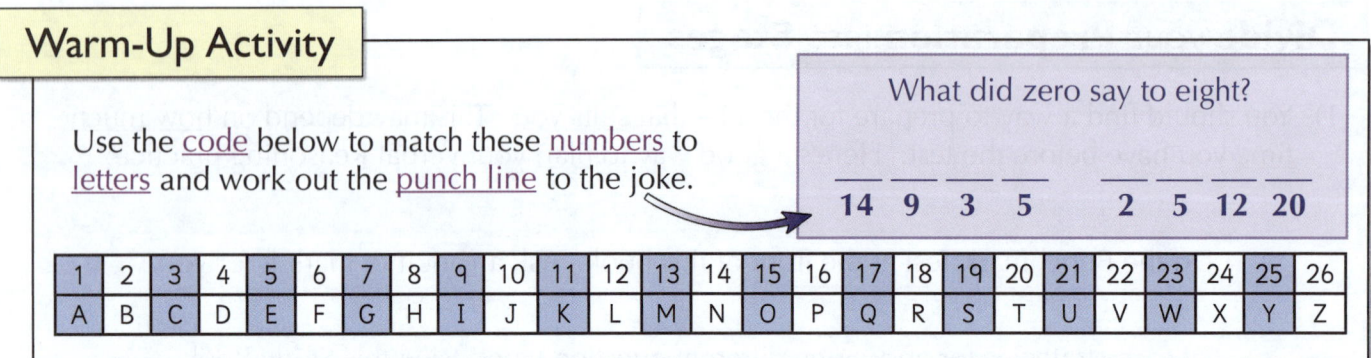

What did zero say to eight?

___ ___ ___ ___   ___ ___ ___ ___
14   9   3   5   2   5 12 20

1	2	3	4	5	6	7	8	9	10	11	12	13	14	15	16	17	18	19	20	21	22	23	24	25	26
A	B	C	D	E	F	G	H	I	J	K	L	M	N	O	P	Q	R	S	T	U	V	W	X	Y	Z

11+ Example Question

Here's an example of the type of question you might get in the test:

Q If the alphabet was written backwards, which letter would be at position 7?

- You need to count forwards or backwards along the alphabet to find the right letter.
- The answer is 't' because it is the seventh letter in the alphabet if you count back from 'z'.

These questions involve Counting Letters

Q What is the alphabet position of the middle letter of the word POMEGRANATE?

Method — Find the middle of the word

1) Some trickier questions might not tell you which letter you have to find the alphabet position of — you have to work it out from the information in the question.

2) First you have to find the middle letter of the word. Count how many letters are in the word, add one then halve the number.

   There are 11 letters in 'pomegranate', so 11 + 1 = 12, 12 ÷ 2 = 6.
   So the middle letter in 'pomegranate' is the sixth letter.

3) Then, count this many letters into the word.

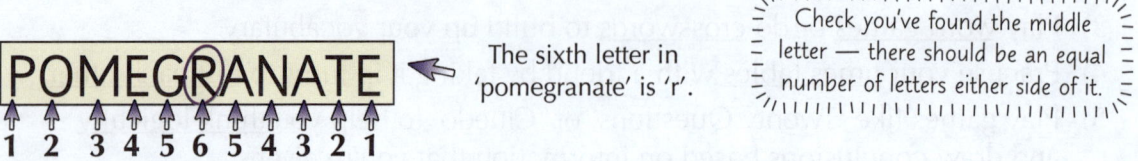

The sixth letter in 'pomegranate' is 'r'.

Check you've found the middle letter — there should be an equal number of letters either side of it.

4) Count along the alphabet to find the number position of the letter 'r' — the answer is 18.

Section One — The Alphabet

Some questions may ask you to **Remove Letters**

 Q If all the letters in the word WOODCHUCK were removed from the alphabet, which letter would be at position 6 of the new alphabet?

Method — Cross out the letters

1) You might be given the alphabet in the test, or you may have to write it out yourself.

When you cross out letters, make sure you use light pencil marks so you can rub them out easily.

2) Cross out all the letters in the word 'woodchuck' from the alphabet.

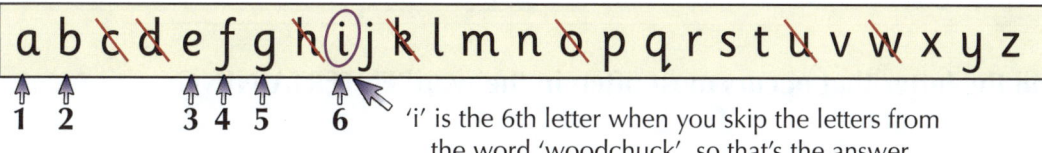

3) Then start at the beginning of the alphabet and count forward 6 letters, skipping the letters that you have crossed out.

'i' is the 6th letter when you skip the letters from the word 'woodchuck', so that's the answer.

 **Tips and Tricks for Alphabet Positions questions**

If you're not given the alphabet in the test then write it out on a spare piece of paper. You'll probably use it several times, so count the letters to make sure there are 26.

Practice Questions

1) Which letter is at the following position in the alphabet:
   a) 8　　　　　　　b) 12　　　　　　　c) 16　　　　　　　d) 22?

2) If the alphabet was written backwards, which letter would be at position:
   a) 9　　　　　　　b) 14　　　　　　　c) 20　　　　　　　d) 24?

3) What is the alphabet position of the middle letter of the word:
   a) PLUNDER　　　　　b) OCTOPUS　　　　　c) RASPBERRY?

4) If all the letters in the word **CANDYFLOSS** were removed from the alphabet, which letter would be at position **12** of the new alphabet?

5) If all the letters in the word **MITTENS** were removed from the alphabet, which letter would be at position **20** of the new alphabet?

Section One — The Alphabet

Identify a Letter From a Clue

Don't be left in the dark — read these pages to become an alphabet ace...

Warm-Up Activity

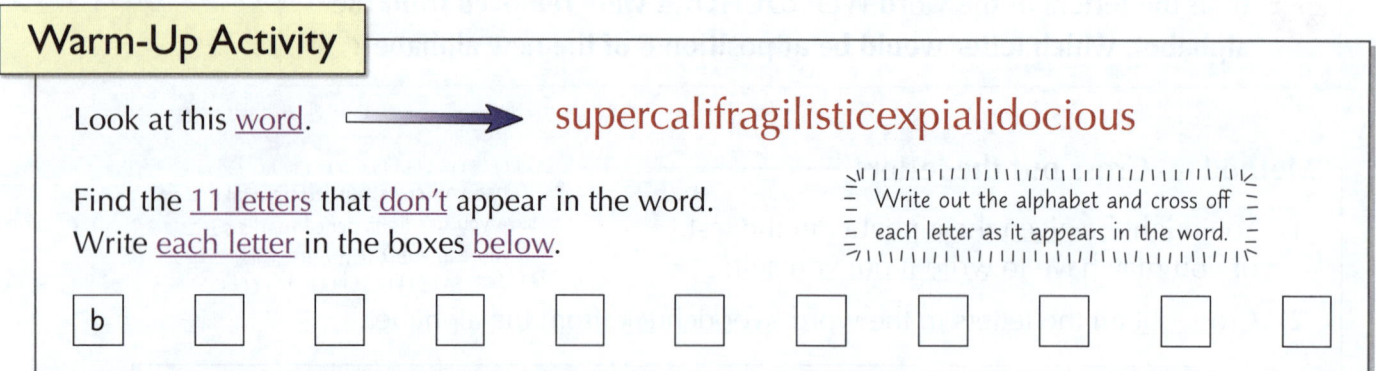

Look at this word. → supercalifragilisticexpialidocious

Find the 11 letters that don't appear in the word.
Write each letter in the boxes below.

Write out the alphabet and cross off each letter as it appears in the word.

| b | | | | | | | | | | |

11+ Example Question

This is the kind of question you might get in the test:

Q Find the letter that occurs most often in the word ENTERTAINING.

- Count each letter that occurs in the word you're given. The letter that appears most is the answer.

Method — Make a chart to help you count

1) Even if you think you can see the answer straight away, use this method to check that you've chosen the right letter.

2) Go through the word and count how many times each letter appears.

'e' appears twice. → ENTERTAINING

It might help to cross off each letter as you count it so you don't accidentally count the same letter twice.

3) Keep count on a piece of paper — drawing a table like the one below is a good idea. The letter with the highest number will be the answer.

'n' is the answer because it occurs more times than any of the other letters.

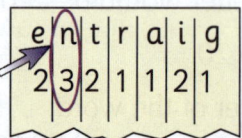

e	n	t	r	a	i	g
2	3	2	1	1	2	1

Make sure you read the question carefully — it won't always ask you to find the letter that appears most often.

Tips and Tricks for Identify a Letter from a Clue questions

Don't waste time thinking about the meaning of the word in the question — you only have to count how many times a letter appears, not understand what the word means.

Section One — The Alphabet

You might have to look at **Several Different Words**

 Find the letter that appears twice in HOBBYHORSE, twice in HOTHOUSE and once in CHOCOLATE.

Method — Count each letter

1) Take the first word. Find the letters that appear twice.

'h', 'o' and 'b' all appear twice — any of these letters could be the answer.

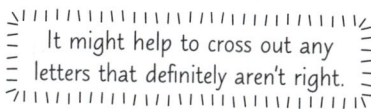

It might help to cross out any letters that definitely aren't right.

2) Look at the second word. Count how many times 'h', 'o' and 'b' appear — you can ignore all the other letters because they don't appear twice in the first word.

Both 'h' and 'o' appear twice again.

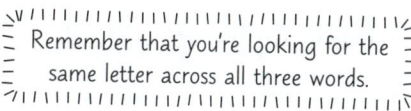

Remember that you're looking for the same letter across all three words.

3) Look at the third word. This time, look for the letter that only appears once in this word, but twice in the other two words. Count how many times 'h' and 'o' appear.

'h' appears once and 'o' appears twice — 'h' is the answer.

 **Tips and Tricks for Identify a Letter from a Clue questions**

If you have to find a letter that occurs in several different words, make sure that you read the question carefully so you know how often the letter appears in each word.

Practice Questions

1) Find the letter that occurs most often in the word:
   a) **NOTORIOUS**   b) **FEBRUARY**   c) **SHIPMENTS**
2) Find the letter that occurs twice in the word:
   a) **SHALLOW**   b) **RESPLENDENT**   c) **HANDCUFFS**
3) Find the letter that occurs twice in **DEADEN**, once in **DANCER** and once in **DANDELION**.

Section One — The Alphabet

Alphabetical Order

You need to know your alphabet upside down and inside out for these questions...

Warm-Up Activity

The first one has been done for you.

Put the words in red into alphabetical order. Write a number from 1 to 12 in the box next to each word to show the order they come in. Use the alphabet to help you.

A B C D E F G H I J K L M N O P Q R S T U V W X Y Z

snake ☐	bison ☐	eagle ☐	aardvark 1	monkey ☐	antelope ☐
meerkat ☐	zebra ☐	tiger ☐	chimp ☐	rhino ☐	bear ☐

11+ Example Question

Here's a sample Alphabetical Order question:

Q If you arrange the following words in alphabetical order, which comes third?

Duller, Dancer, Dangle, Danger, Dinner

- Put the words in alphabetical order — if the words start with the same first letter, you'll need to look at the rest of the letters in order.

Method — Look at each letter in turn

1) Look at the first letter of each word to see if this will help you put the words in order.

Duller, Dancer, Dangle, Danger, Dinner ➾ They all begin with 'd', so this doesn't help you.

2) Look at the next letter. Work through the words letter by letter until you find the answer.

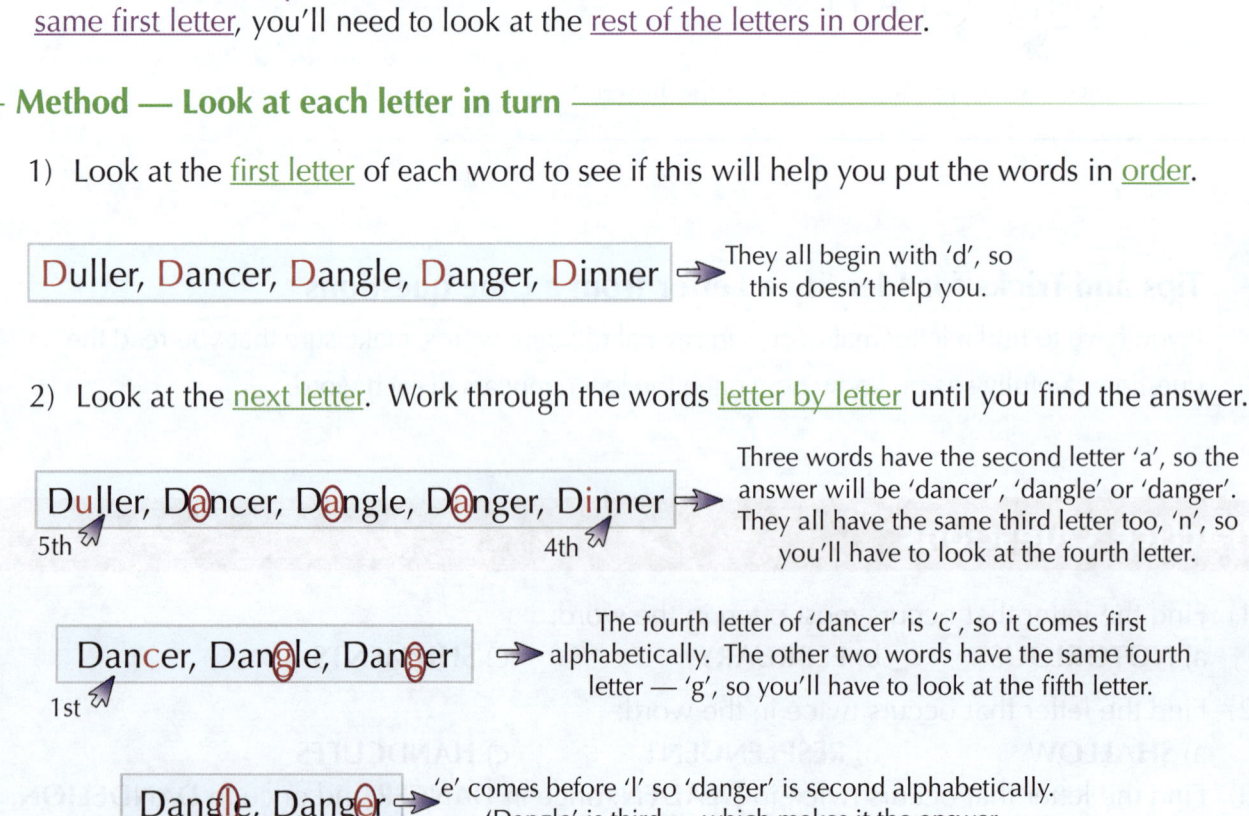

Duller (5th), Dancer, Dangle, Danger, Dinner (4th) ➾ Three words have the second letter 'a', so the answer will be 'dancer', 'dangle' or 'danger'. They all have the same third letter too, 'n', so you'll have to look at the fourth letter.

Dancer (1st), Dangle, Danger ➾ The fourth letter of 'dancer' is 'c', so it comes first alphabetically. The other two words have the same fourth letter — 'g', so you'll have to look at the fifth letter.

Dangle (3rd), Danger (2nd) ➾ 'e' comes before 'l' so 'danger' is second alphabetically. 'Dangle' is third — which makes it the answer.

Look at the last letter first for **Backwards** questions

 Q If you spell the following words backwards, then put them in alphabetical order, which comes second?

Rapidly, Cleverly, Spooky, Happily, Unkindly

Method — Look at the end of the word

1) Look at the <u>last letter</u> of each word to help you start putting the words in <u>alphabetical order</u>.

   Rapidl**y**, Cleverl**y**, Spook**y**, Happil**y**, Unkindl**y** ⇒ All the words end with 'y', so you'll need to look at more of the letters.

2) Take the <u>next letter back</u> from the <u>end</u> of each word and <u>work backwards</u> until you can <u>answer</u> the question.

   'Spooky' has 'k' as the second letter back, and 'k' comes before 'l'. So 'spooky' would come first alphabetically. ⇒ Rapid(l)y, Cleve(rl)y, Spoo(k)y, Happi(l)y, Unkind(l)y
   1st

   Rapi(d)ly, Cleve(rl)y, Happi(l)y, Unkin(d)ly ⇒ 'Rapidly' and 'unkindly' both have 'd' as the third letter back, and 'd' comes before 'i' and 'r' in the alphabet. So one of these words will be the answer.
   5th   4th

   'Rapidly' has 'i' as the fourth letter back, whereas 'unkindly' has 'n' as the fourth letter back. 'Rapidly' would be second written backwards — so that's the answer. ⇒ Rap(i)dly, Unki(n)dly
   2nd   3rd

Practice Questions

1) If you arrange the following words in alphabetical order, which comes second?

   Sparse, Spears, Spaces, Sporty, Spring

2) If you arrange the following words in alphabetical order, which comes fourth?

   Confuse, Confides, Confront, Confine, Conference

3) If you spell the following words backwards, then put them in alphabetical order, which word comes second?

   Unstable, Vegetable, Comfortable, Constable, Unflappable

4) If you spell the following words backwards, then put them in alphabetical order, which comes third?

   Irate, Complicate, Deliberate, Frustrate, Inmate

Section One — The Alphabet

Section Two — Making Words

Preparing for the Test

Make sure you know how words are made — it'll help you to do well with these questions.

Making Words Questions test your Spelling

The questions in this section will test your word recognition and your spelling skills. You can improve these skills in a couple of ways:

1) Read lots of books — make sure you look up any words that you don't recognise.
2) Ask friends or family to give you regular spelling tests — keep a record of any words that you get wrong so they can test you again next time.
3) Play word games like SCRABBLE® or do crosswords and wordsearches.

Lots of words follow Spelling Rules

Whether you're solving an anagram or looking for hidden words, it'll help if you can recognise common spelling patterns that occur in words.

Patterns at the Start of words

1) Words can start with any letter of the alphabet, but not any combination.
2) You'll see 'b', 'c', 'f', 'g', 'p' or 't' before 'l' or 'r', but never after 'l' or 'r' at the start of a word.

   blow, crown, flip, grab, plot, trip

   lb✗ rb✗ lc✗ rc✗ lf✗ rf✗ lg✗ rg✗ lp✗ rp✗ rt✗

3) 'h' is common after 'c', 's', 't' and 'w'. ⇒ chip, shop, this, when

4) A prefix can be added to the start of a word to change its meaning, for example:

   un- (unlock, untidy)   dis- (disappear, dislike)   in- (inedible, indescribable)

Patterns in the Middle of words

1) Almost all words contain vowels. Some patterns of vowels appear frequently, e.g.

   ee oo ou ie ea   seen look pout diet tear

2) Some vowels rarely appear together, e.g. 'uo', 'iu', 'ae'.

3) Double consonants in the middle of words are common — you'll often come across 'tt', 'ss' or 'pp', but it's less likely you'll see a word with 'hh', 'vv', 'jj', 'ww' or 'xx'.

   butter assume stopping

4) If you can recognise common vowel and consonant patterns that appear in the middle of words, such as 'per', 'our', 'are' and 'ate', it'll help to improve your spelling.

Section Two — Making Words

Patterns at the **End** of words

1) Some combinations of consonants are often found at the end of words. For example:

   chur**ch** clo**ck** fif**th** ca**sh** har**m** hi**gh** **str**ing

2) Suffixes come at the end of words — they can be verb endings like '-ed', plurals such as '-s' or adverb endings like '-ly'. Here are some common suffixes:

   -**ition** (add**ition**)   -**ity** (humid**ity**)   -**ful** (care**ful**)   -**ing** (play**ing**)   -**y** (sand**y**)

3) Remember, when you add a suffix the spelling of the root word can change:

   take ⇒ take**ing** ✗ tak**ing** ✓   prepare ⇒ prepar**eation** ✗ prepar**ation** ✓

Use **Spelling Patterns** to help you answer questions

1) If you know a bit about prefixes it can help you work out the meaning of words, for example:

   preexists → pre → 'pre' is a prefix that means 'before'.
             → exists → 'exists' is a word that means 'alive'.

   If you don't recognise a word, try breaking it down.

   So by understanding prefixes, you could make a sensible guess that 'preexists' means 'to be alive before something else'.

2) Learn some common patterns in the middle of words — it'll help with your spelling.

   run ⇒ ru**nn**ing   row ⇒ ro**w**ing

   If you can recognise that double 'n' in the middle of words is common, but double 'w' isn't, it'll help you to spell words correctly.

3) Think about word endings to help you to solve anagrams.

   TTASNIO ← If you recognise that the anagram contains the ending 'tion', it's easier to work out that it spells 'station'.

Practice Questions

1) Find three prefixes other than un-, dis- and in-.
2) Can you think of any words that start with the following letters?
   a) str   b) blr   c) shr   d) ds
3) Unscramble the following anagrams:
   a) YZCAR   b) IGNMXI   c) NTALEMECP

Section Two — Making Words

Missing Letters

Some letters have gone missing. Looks like another excuse for a Verbal Reasoning question.

Warm-Up Activity

Look at this word chain.  garagechordereceiptokenetball

The letters in red are 'linking letters' — the last letter of one word is the first letter of the next. Write down your own chain to link the words brain and melt — make it as long as you can.

11+ Example Question

Here's a sample 11+ style question:

 **Find the letter that will finish the first word and start the second word of each pair. The same letter must be used for both pairs.**

gri (__) ain   sea (__) ale

- You need to add the same letter to both sets of brackets to make four new words.

Method 1 — Brainstorming

1) Read the question. Take the first set and think of some four-letter words that start with 'gri_'.

   gri (__) ain ⇒ grid   grim   grin   grip   grit

   'd', 'm', 'n', 'p' and 't' can all be added to 'gri_' to make a new word.

2) Add 'd', 'm', 'n', 'p' and 't' to the start of _ain to try and make a new word. ⇒ dain ✗   main ✓   nain ✗   pain ✓   tain ✗

3) So 'm' and 'p' work for the first set — they make the words 'gri(m)ain' and 'gri(p)ain'.

4) Only one letter will work for both sets, so you need to try both letters in the second set.

   sea (m) ale ✓ ← 'm' makes the words 'seam' and 'male'.

   sea (p) ale ✗ ← 'p' makes the word 'pale' but 'seap' isn't a word.

5) 'm' works with all four words, so that's the answer.

 **Tips and Tricks for Missing Letters questions**

Missing Letters questions are a bit easier on a multiple choice test — the answer can **only** be one of the letters you've been given. Try each option on your answer sheet to see which one works.

Section Two — Making Words

Try each letter in the **Alphabet**

Key Question **Q** loo (_) ite   lea (_) ill

Method 2 — Going through the alphabet

1) If you can't think of a letter that works for all the words, and you don't have the multiple-choice options to help you narrow the answer down, try each letter of the alphabet in turn.

2) If you have a spare piece of paper, it may help to write the alphabet lengthways down the side.

3) Take the first word, run the alphabet strip alongside the word with the missing letter and jot down any combinations that work.

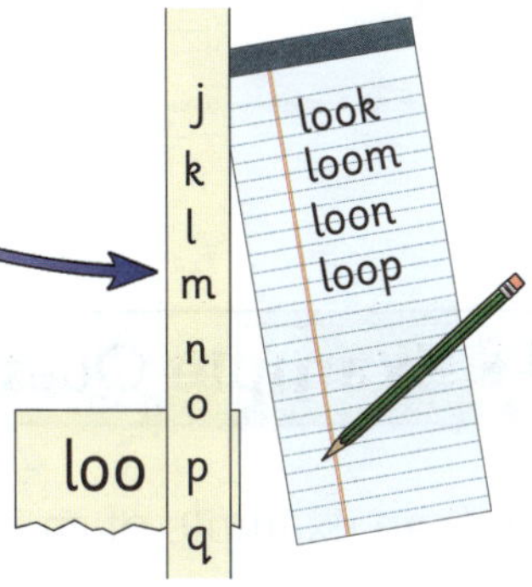

look✓ loom✓ loon✓ loop✓ loot✓

The letters 'k', 'm', 'n', 'p' and 't' can be added to the end of 'loo_' to make a new word.

4) Once you have a list of letters that complete 'loo_', try them with '_ite'.

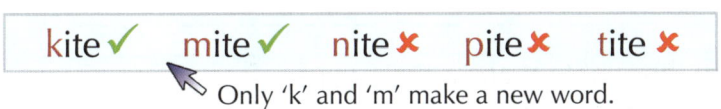

kite✓   mite✓   nite✗   pite✗   tite✗

Only 'k' and 'm' make a new word.

Watch out for words that sound like real words, but are spelled incorrectly, like 'tite'.

5) Try the remaining letters in the second pair of words.

lea (**k**) ill ✓   'leak' and 'kill' are both words.

lea (**m**) ill ✗   'mill' is a word, but 'leam' isn't — 'm' isn't the answer.

6) 'k' works with all four words, so that's the answer.

Practice Questions

1) Find the letter that will finish the first word and start the second word.
   a) cal (_) lap   b) to (_) ou   c) to (_) lf   d) sli (_) ix

2) Find the letter that will finish the first word and start the second word of each pair. The same letter must be used for both pairs.
   a) do (_) ap   plu (_) ram   b) wa (_) oon   mis (_) un

Section Two — Making Words

Move a Letter

Move a Letter questions test how well you can recognise words — read on for some handy methods.

Warm-Up Activity

Look at the words below.
For each word, remove one letter to make a new word.
The letters you remove will spell out a secret message.

We've done the first one for you — take the 'c' from the word 'cash' to give the word 'ash'.

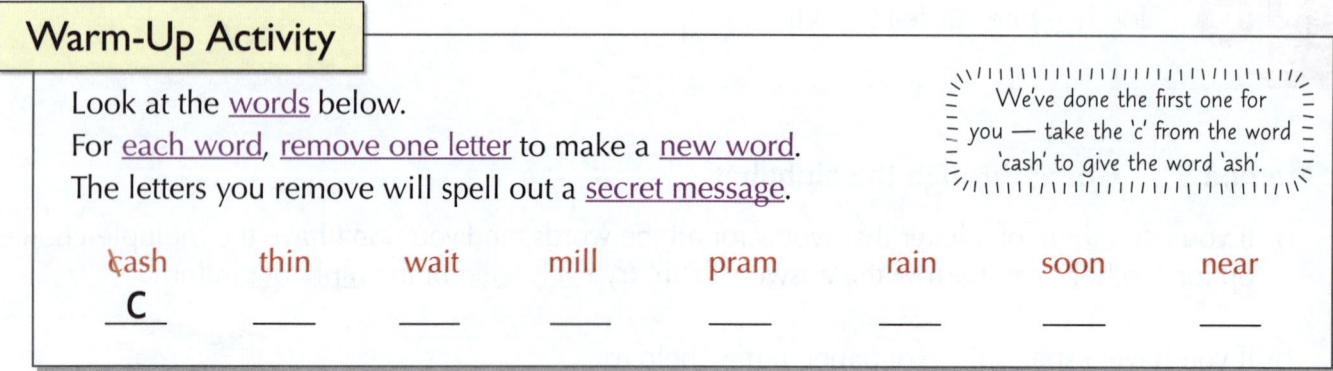

cash	thin	wait	mill	pram	rain	soon	near
c							

11+ Example Question

Here's an example of an 11+ style question you might find on the test:

> **Q** Remove one letter from the first word and add it to the second word to make two new words. Do not change the order of the other letters.
>
> brown   law

- You need to remove a letter from 'brown' to make a new word and add the same letter to 'law' to make a new word.

Method 1 — Cover each letter

1) Look at the first word. Cover each letter in turn to see if you can make a new word by removing a letter.

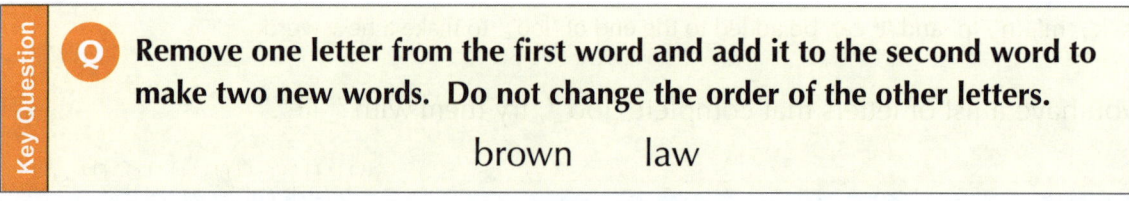

brown → rown ✗ bown ✗ brwn ✗ bron ✗ brow ✓ → n

← This is the only letter that can be removed and still leave a real word.

2) Try adding the letter 'n' to the word 'law' to make a new word.

law → n → nlaw ✗ lnaw ✗ lanw ✗ lawn ✓

← 'lawn' is the only word that can be made.

The letter could be added to the **beginning**, **middle** or **end** of the second word, so you need to try the letter in all the different positions.

3) So 'n' is the letter that moves, and the new words are 'brow' and 'lawn'.

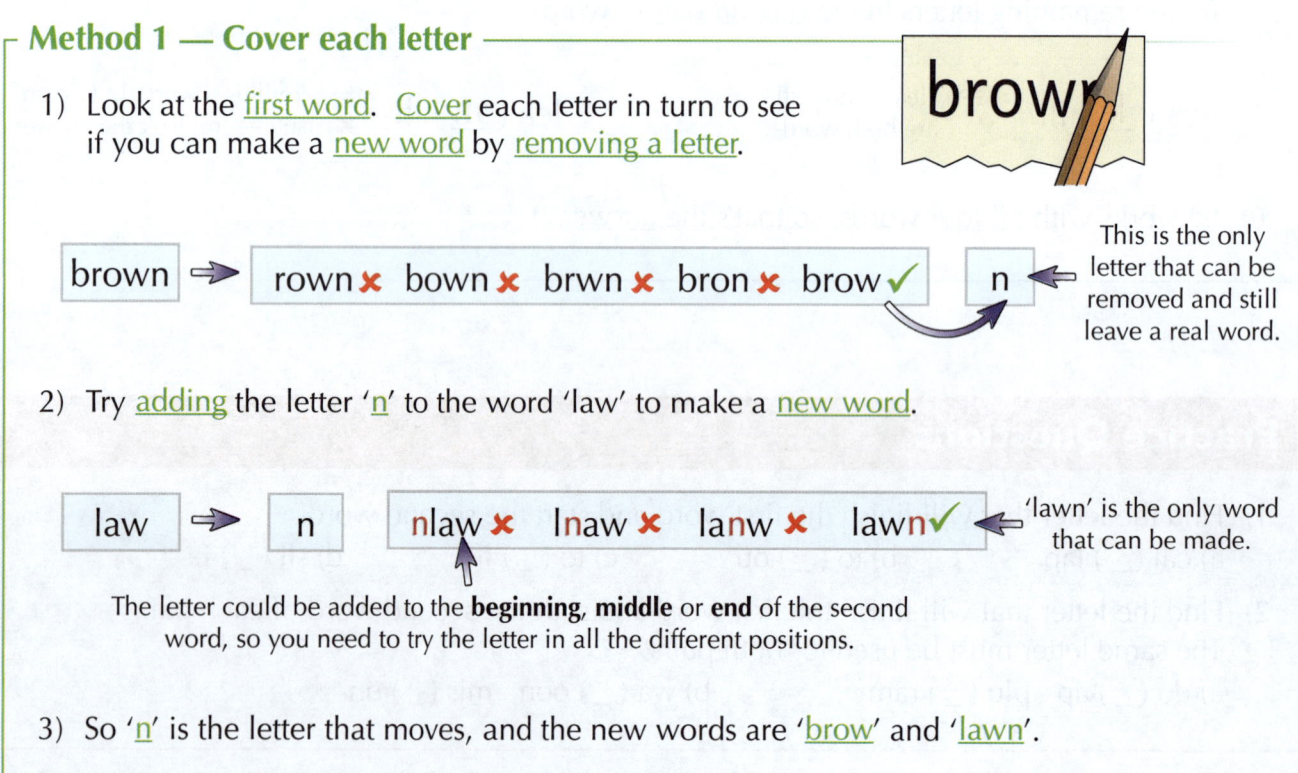

Section Two — Making Words

Sometimes you might get a Trickier Question

Key Question

Q Remove one letter from the first word and add it to the second word to make two new words. Do not change the order of the other letters.

plain   cap

Method 2 — Trial and error

1) Sometimes, you might be able to make <u>more than one</u> word by <u>removing different letters</u> from the first word.

2) Look at the <u>first word</u>. <u>Cover</u> each letter in turn to see if you can make a <u>new word</u> by <u>removing a letter</u>.

plain → lain ✓   pain ✓   plin ✗   plan ✓   plai ✗

p   l   i ← These are the letters that can be removed and still leave a real word.

3) Try each of these letters with 'cap' to see if it makes a <u>new word</u>. <u>Only one</u> of the letters should work.

cap → p	pcap ✗ cpap ✗ capp ✗ capp ✗
cap → l	lcap ✗ clap ✓ calp ✗ capl ✗
cap → i	icap ✗ ciap ✗ caip ✗ capi ✗

4) So '<u>l</u>' is the letter that moves, and the new words are '<u>pain</u>' and '<u>clap</u>'.

Tips and Tricks for Move a Letter questions

If you're unsure whether you've made a correctly spelled new word, try comparing it to words that you already know. So in this example, 'clap' looks similar to words such as 'slap' and 'flap'.

Practice Questions

Remove one letter from the first word and add it to the second word to make two new words. Do not change the order of the other letters.

1) clone   gad   2) split   eel

3) pride   air   4) crook   cow

5) clean   cap   6) wheat   sell

Section Two — Making Words

16

Hidden Word

Get yourself ready for some Hidden Word questions — find the words to earn the marks.

Warm-Up Activity

Write down two new words, for which the letters of the word in red sit across the end of one word and the start of the next.

The first one has been done for you.

took ⇒ __too__   __kind__   leap ⇒ _____ _____   ball ⇒ _____ _____

earn ⇒ _____ _____   hand ⇒ _____ _____   chin ⇒ _____ _____

11+ Example Question

This is an example of the sort of Hidden Word question you can expect to find in the test:

Key Question

Q **In the sentence below a four-letter word is hidden at the end of one word and the start of the next. Find the pair of words which contains the hidden word.**

Don't forget to clean each one twice.

- Spot a pair of words that have a word hidden at the end of one word and the start of the next.

Method 1 — Look at the vowels

1) Read the sentence and identify all the words that begin or end with vowels.

Don't forget to clean each one twice.

It's almost certain that the hidden word will have a vowel in it, so looking at the words that start or end with vowels can help you find it quickly.

2) If the word ends with a vowel, take the word to its right and look for the hidden word.

to clean ⇒ tocl ✗   ocle ✗   Neither of these are real words, so move on to the next pair.

3) If the word starts with a vowel, take the word to its left and look for the hidden word.

clean each ⇒ eane ✗   anea ✗   neac ✗   None of these are real words, so move on to the next pair.

4) If the word starts and ends with a vowel, take the word to its left and right and look for the hidden word.

each one twice ⇒ acho ✗   chon ✗   hone ✓   onet ✗   netw ✗   etwi ✗

'hone' is a real word. So the answer is 'each one'.

Section Two — Making Words

Check each **Pair Of Words**

Key Question **Q** Dave hates lumpy powdered custard.

Method 2 — Rule out options one by one

1) If looking at the vowels <u>doesn't work</u>, look at each pair of words in turn — start with the <u>first two words</u>.

   > Dave hates

   You won't have time to write out all the combinations in the test, so use two pencils to cover up the letters either side of the four letters you're looking at.

2) Look at:
   - The <u>last three letters</u> of the first word, and the <u>first letter</u> of the second word. ⇒ aveh ✗
   - The <u>last two letters</u> of the first word and the <u>first two letters</u> of the second word. ⇒ veha ✗
   - The <u>last letter</u> of the first word, and the <u>first three letters</u> of the second word. ⇒ ehat ✗

   None of these combinations make a word.

3) If the first pair of words <u>doesn't work</u>, move on to the <u>second</u> and <u>third</u> words in the sentence and <u>repeat</u> the process.

   > hates lumpy ⇒ tesl ✗   eslu ✗   slum ✓   ⇐ 'slum' is a word.

4) There should only be <u>one correct answer</u>, so the hidden word is '<u>slum</u>' and the answer is '<u>hates lumpy</u>'.

TIPS & TRICKS

Tips and Tricks for Hidden Word questions

If you look at all the possible combinations and still can't find the hidden word, pick the option that seems the most sensible. Even if you don't recognise the word 'slum', it looks a lot more possible than combinations like 'aveh' or 'eslu'.

Practice Questions

In each sentence below a four-letter word is hidden at the end of one word and the start of the next. Find the hidden four-letter word.

1) The turnip eaten yesterday was unripe.
2) Rebecca keeps slugs in her room.
3) Mr Gregory also farms wheat.
4) I like my placid old dog.
5) His banjo keeps me up at night.
6) My burger is covered in cheese.

Section Two — Making Words

Find the Missing Word

You'll need a good vocab and an understanding of how words are made to answer these questions.

Warm-Up Activity

1) Look at the letters in red below.
2) You've got 30 seconds per letter to write down as many three-letter words as you can that start with each letter. Ask a parent or friend to time you.

P   S   A   T   M

11+ Example Question

Take a look at the question below — it's the sort of thing you can expect in the test.

> **Find the three-letter word that completes the word in capital letters, and so finishes the sentence in a sensible way.**
>
> There was a **TREDOUS** bang when the washing machine exploded.

- You need to add a three-letter word to **TREDOUS** to make a word which finishes the sentence.

Method 1 — Look at the word type

1) Read the sentence. Think about the word in capitals and what sort of word would make sense in the context of the sentence.

> There was a **TREDOUS** bang when the washing machine exploded.

It looks like the missing word is describing the noun 'bang', so it must be an adjective.

It's describing the sound of a washing machine exploding so the adjective might mean 'loud' or 'big'.

2) Look at the word in capitals again. You need to find an adjective that means 'loud' or 'big', that is ten letters long and that contains the letters **TREDOUS**.

TREMENDOUS ← 'Tremendous' is an adjective that means 'big' that is 10 letters long.

3) Check that the word makes sense in the sentence.

There was a **TREMENDOUS** bang when the washing machine exploded. ✓

4) Check that the missing letters makes a three-letter word.

TREMENDOUS ⇒ The missing three letters spell 'men', so that's your answer.

Section Two — Making Words

Use **Prefixes** and **Suffixes** to help you work out the answer

Key Question

Q The complicated film **CONFD** me.

Method 2 — Think about the order of the letters

Have a look at p.10 for a reminder of letters that don't go together.

1) Look at the word in capitals. Try to identify any combinations of letters that don't look right.

   The complicated film **CONFD** me.

   'CON' looks sensible — it's found in words like 'contain', 'contour', 'concern'.

   The complicated film **CONFD** me.

   'NFD' looks less recognisable. There are three consonants together. Looks like there's a vowel or two missing...

2) Once you've identified the part of the word that looks strange, think about the word type and whether that gives you any clues to what the missing word could be.

   The complicated film **CONFD** me.

   There aren't any verbs in the sentence, so the word in capitals must be a **verb**. The word in capitals ends in 'D', so the word could be in the past tense. That would mean that there's an 'e' missing from the 'ed' ending.

   It may help you to write the word out with gaps where you think the missing letters go.

   CONF _ _ E D

3) Try to think of some eight-letter verbs that start with 'conf' and end with 'ed'.

   conf**id**ed   conf**in**ed   conf**us**ed

   'confided' and 'confined' are both words, but the missing letters 'ide' and 'ine' don't spell new words.

   'confused' is a real word and the missing letters spell the word 'use'.

4) Put the complete word into the sentence to check that it makes sense.

   The complicated film **CONFUSED** me. ✓

   'confused' makes sense in the context of the sentence, so the answer is 'use'.

Practice Questions

Find the three-letter word that completes the word in capital letters, and so finishes the sentence in a sensible way.

1) The teacher **FNED** at the naughty child.
2) The **TENS** lapped at a saucer of milk.
3) We **GLSED** a deer running through the trees.

Section Two — Making Words

20

Use a Rule to Make a Word

This question type can be one of the trickier ones on the paper — don't worry, we've got it covered...

Warm-Up Activity

Look at the words in the box. Draw a line between each pair of words that use the same letters.

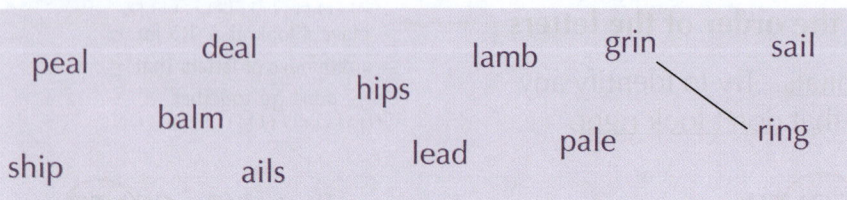

The first one has been done for you to start you off.

11+ Example Question

Here's an example of the sort of question that you might see in the test:

 **The words in the second set follow the same pattern as the words in the first set. Find the missing word to complete the second set.**

sag (sat) rut   but (?) fog

- Find the letters taken from the outer words in the first set to make the word in brackets.
- You need to use the same pattern to work out the answer to the second set of words.

Method 1 — Spot the pattern

1) Look at the first group of words. Take the word in brackets, and identify the letters that also appear in the two outer words.

's' and 'a' appear at the start of the left-hand word. →    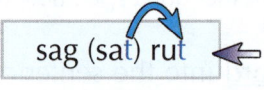 ← The letter 't' appears at the end of the right-hand word.

2) Identify the pattern which has been applied to the two outer words to make the word in brackets. ⇨ Put the **first two letters** of the **left-hand word** together with the **last letter** of the **right-hand word**.

3) Apply the pattern to the second set of words.

 ← Using the same pattern as the first set of words, the word 'bug' is made.

Make sure you mark the right choice on your answer sheet. There may be some similar words designed to trick you.

4) Check that your answer is a real word and is the same length as the word in the first set of brackets.

5) If you're using a multiple-choice answer sheet, your answer should be one of the five options.

Section Two — Making Words

Write down the options for Each Letter

Key Question  rely (yell) tale   scum (?) mane

Method 2 — Write down what each letter could be

1) If a letter from the word in brackets appears <u>more than once in the outer words</u>, you'll need to use a <u>different method</u> to help you answer the question.

'e' and 'l' appear in both of the outer words.

2) <u>Identify</u> which letter has been <u>taken</u> from the <u>outer words</u> to make the first letter of the <u>word in brackets</u>.

3) Find the <u>equivalent letter</u> in the second set.

4) Move on to the <u>next letter</u>. If a letter appears in <u>both</u> of the outer words, <u>write down</u> both the <u>equivalent letters</u> from the second set.

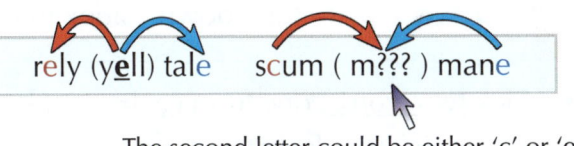

The second letter could be either 'c' or 'e'.

5) <u>Repeat</u> this method until you've written down the <u>possible letters</u> for <u>each</u> letter position of the <u>word</u>.

6) There should only be <u>one combination</u> of letters that makes a <u>new word</u> — so the answer for this question is '<u>menu</u>'.

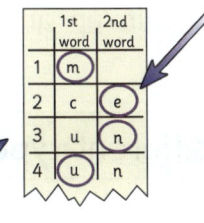

 **Tips and Tricks for Use a Rule to Make a Word questions**

If you're doing a multiple-choice test, use the five choices to help you. If you can work out one or two letters, that might be enough to work out the answer, or at least rule out a couple of options.

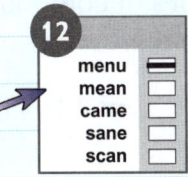

Practice Questions

The words in the second set follow the same pattern as the words in the first set.
Find the missing word to complete the second set.

1) tap (pod) nod   son (?) rib   2) deal (ode) crop   spin (?) load

3) poet (port) part   wept (?) stag   4) flow (glow) logs   earl (?) ripe

Section Two — Making Words

Compound Words

Compound words are made up of two separate words joined together — like 'milkshake'.

Warm-Up Activity

1) For each of the words below, write down as many compound words as you can in one minute.
2) For example, for the word 'house' you might make words such as 'lighthouse' or 'housemaid'.

house   bird   in   night   down

11+ Example Question

This is what a Compound Words question might look like:

> **Q** **Underline a word from the first set, followed by a word from the second set, that go together to form a new word.**
>
> (up   down   side)   (back   front   forward)

- Pick two words, one from each set of brackets, that make a new word when they're combined.
- Don't pick words that go together, e.g. 'fish' and 'chips', or hyphenated words such as 'full-time'.
- The correct pair, 'up' and 'front', can be combined to make the new word 'upfront'.

There are different types of Compound Words

The Pronunciation of some compounds Won't Change

These compounds are the easiest to spot, and should be the types of compounds you come across most often in the test. Here are some examples:

The pronunciation for both parts of the compound stays the same.

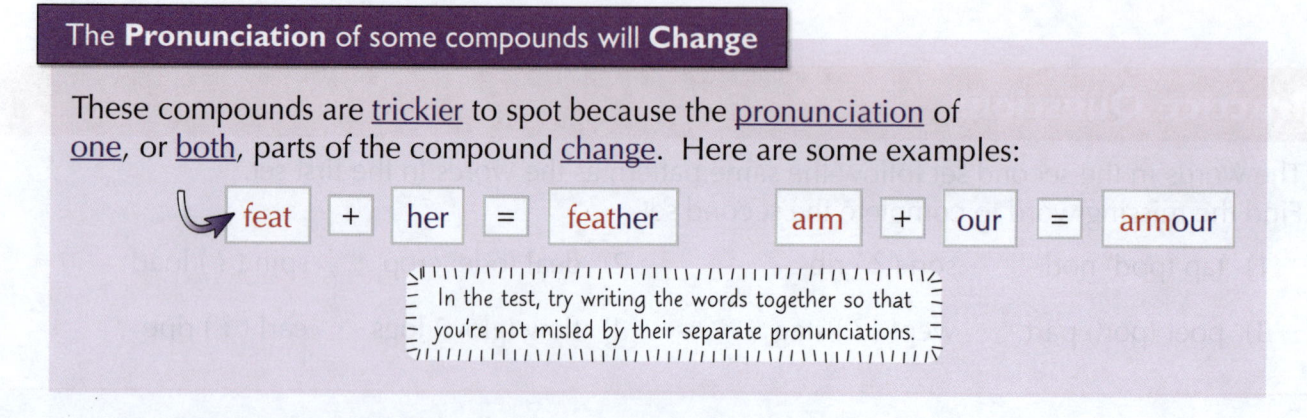

blackbird   update   below   antelope

The Pronunciation of some compounds will Change

These compounds are trickier to spot because the pronunciation of one, or both, parts of the compound change. Here are some examples:

feat + her = feather   arm + our = armour

In the test, try writing the words together so that you're not misled by their separate pronunciations.

Section Two — Making Words

Try pairs of words together One By One

Key Question (park sleep mass) (per age king)

Method — Rule out the options that don't work

1) Take the <u>first word</u> from the <u>first set of brackets</u> and try <u>combining</u> it with each word in the <u>second set of brackets</u> to see whether it makes a <u>new word</u>.

| parkper ✗ | parkage ✗ | parkking ✗ |

'parkking' sounds as if it could be right, but it's not spelled correctly.

2) If the first word doesn't make a new word, take the <u>second word</u> in the <u>first bracket</u> and <u>repeat</u> the process.

| sleepper ✗ | sleepage ✗ | sleepking ✗ |

For a bit more on common double letters, turn back to p.10.

'sleepper' sounds OK when you say it aloud, but when you write the word as a compound, it isn't spelt correctly.

3) Try the <u>last word</u> in the <u>first bracket</u> and <u>repeat</u> the process.

| massper ✗ | massage ✓ | massking ✗ |

'massking' sounds as if it could be right, but it's got an 's' too many.

Separately, 'mass' and 'age' don't sound like they make a new word, but when you write them down they make a word — 'massage'.

4) So the correct answer is '<u>massage</u>'.

Tips and Tricks for Compound Words questions

Another type of Compound Words question will ask you to find a word that can go **before** or **after** a set of words. So you might have to think of a word that can go after 'net', 'foot' and 'meat' to make three new words. The answer to this question would be 'ball'.

Practice Questions

Choose a word from the first set, followed by a word from the second set, that go together to form a new word.

1) (pat rib rot)   (tin ten bin)   2) (am be is)   (wear ware were)

3) (drag pull push) (in on an)   4) (clot clog clump) (her he she)

Section Two — Making Words

Complete a Word Pair

These questions are easier than they look — especially when you have a foolproof method.

Warm-Up Activity

1) Look at this word in red ➡ **SUPERINTENDENT**
2) Write down as many words as you can using any combination of letters from the word in one minute.

Challenge family and friends to beat your score.

| 0-5 words — Try Again! | 6-10 words — OK | 11-16 — Nice Work! | 17+ words — Word Wizard! |

11+ Example Question

Here's an example of a Complete a Word Pair question:

 Find the word that completes the third pair of words so that it follows the same pattern as the first two pairs.

marks arm   ready ear   glove (?)

- All three pairs of words are formed using the same pattern — you need to work out what the pattern is, and apply it to the third pair to work out the answer.
- The answer is 'log' — remove the last two letters, then move the first letter to the end of the word.

There are different types of Pattern

Removing, rearranging and changing letters

1) You might be asked to remove and rearrange letters, e.g.:

    mint tin   bows sow   hips (__sip__)

The first letter of each pair has been removed and then the last letter has been moved to the front.

2) You might have to spot words that have been written backwards, e.g.:

    emit time   keep peek   rats (__star__)

3) You might have to change a letter, e.g.:

    jump lump   dine fine   rail (__tail__)

The first letter of each word moves along the alphabet two letters each time.

    bile bite   male mate   vole (__vote__)

The 'l' changes to a 't' in each pair.

Section Two — Making Words

Use the Most Helpful Pair of Words

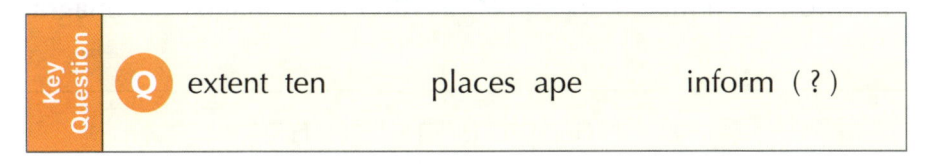

Key Question

Q extent ten   places ape   inform (?)

Method 1 — Spot the pattern

1) Look at the first pair. Check if any of the letters in the second word are repeated in the first word. In the first pair, the letters 't' and 'e' are each used twice.

2) If there are repeated letters, don't waste time trying to solve the first pair — move on to the next pair to see if the pattern is more obvious.

   places ape ← There are no repeated letters — each of the letters in the second word only appears once in the first word.

3) To find the answer you need to take the first, third and fifth letters of 'inform' and arrange them in the order 3rd, 1st, 5th. So the answer is 'fir'.

Key Question

Q cabbages sage   wandered dare   focussed (?)

Method 2 — Solve the letters that aren't repeated first

1) Harder questions may have repeated letters in both words.

2) Look at both pairs — the first pair has fewer repeated letters, so use that. Discount any letters that don't appear in the second word. → cabbages sage

3) Discount the same letters in the third word.   focussed ← The first, third and fourth letters of 'cabbages' don't appear in 'sage', so you can discount these letters in 'focussed'.

4) Rearrange the letters in the same pattern as the first pair of words. Leave a gap if you're unsure of a letter. → d __ se

5) If you get most of the word you'll often be able to guess the missing letter. Here, the only letter that fills the gap to make a word is 'o', so the answer is 'dose'. → dose

Practice Questions

Find the word that completes the third pair of words so that it follows the same pattern as the first two pairs.

1) writer rite   shandy hand   tables (?)   2) mobile lob   barber ear   ration (?)

3) fabric cab   jetsam met   caters (?)   4) mammoth ham   million nil   matador (?)

Section Two — Making Words

Anagram in a Sentence

Anagrams are when the letters in a word are all mixed up, so NAAAMRG is an anagram of anagram.

Warm-Up Activity

Reorder the anagrams and write the answers into the crossword.

DOWN
1. YRMA
2. GLENVIA
3. UMEN
4. GUOYN

ACROSS
1. WOL
2. EEYVR
3. ~~LVEUA~~
4. MNII
5. NIRG

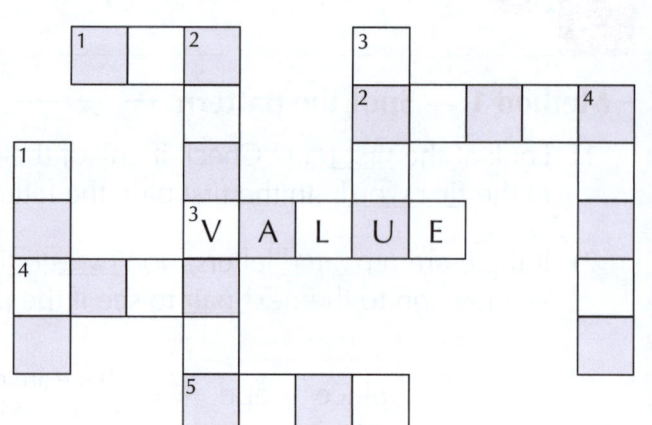

11+ Example Question

Here's an example of an Anagram in a Sentence question:

> **Q** Rearrange the letters in capitals to spell a word that completes the sentence in a sensible way.
>
> The **YGEDER** chicken ate all the corn.

- You need to unjumble the letters to form a word that makes sense.

Method 1 — Write the letters out in a circle

1) Read the sentence and look at the anagram.

   The **YGEDER** chicken ate all the corn.

   If you're struggling to see the word, keep rearranging the letters.

2) If you don't recognise the word straight away, try writing the letters out in a circle to help you spot the word.

   You may spot that 'g' and 'r' are often found at the start of words, 'ee' often occurs in the middle, and 'y' is most likely to be found at the end of words.

   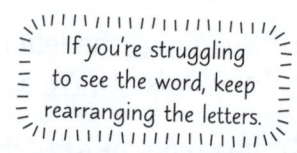

3) Once you think you've found the answer, try it in the sentence to check that it makes sense.

   The **GREEDY** chicken ate all the corn. ✓ ⇒ So the answer is 'greedy'.

Section Two — Making Words

Try to spot common **Letter Patterns**

 I was **NHISUTOG** when I lost my voice.

Method 2 — Think about the word type

1) Read the sentence. Think about what word type the anagram could belong to.

I was **NHISUTOG** when I lost my voice. → The anagram comes after 'was', so it's likely to be a **verb**. Verbs that follow 'was' often end in 'ed' or 'ing'.

I was **NHISUTOG** when I lost my voice.

The anagram doesn't contain the letters 'ed' but it does contain the letters 'ing', so we can try rearranging the anagram with 'ing' at the end. → **HSUTOING**

2) Look at the rest of the sentence to try and find a clue about the meaning of the anagram.

I was **NHISUTOG** when I lost my voice. → The sentence is about someone who has lost their voice — you lose your voice when you talk a lot or shout.

3) You've worked out that the word is likely to mean 'making a lot of noise', so look at the remaining letters with 'ing' removed to see if words like 'talk', 'shout' 'yell' etc fit.

HSUTO → **SHOUT** → I was **SHOUTING** when I lost my voice. ✓

 **Tips and Tricks for Anagram in a Sentence questions**

When you're solving an anagram, use the rest of the sentence to help you work out whether it's a noun, verb, adjective or adverb. Try to spot any prefixes or suffixes that are related to that word type, such as 'tion' or 'ment' for nouns, then unscramble the rest of the word.

Practice Questions

Rearrange the letters in capitals to spell a word that completes the sentence in a sensible way.

1) My aunty has five nieces and **WHSEPNE**.
2) It was quite **LCODUY** and cold when we went to the park.
3) I ordered **NEGSLAA** for dinner when I went to the Italian restaurant.
4) He walked **CFURAEYLL** along the tightrope.
5) We visited a **NGLESHI** beach on holiday.

Section Two — Making Words

Word Ladders

Word Ladders — your stairway to success....

Warm-Up Activity

Continue this word chain by changing one letter at a time to make a new word.

team ⇒ _seam_ ⇒ _seal_ ⇒ _____ ⇒ _____ ⇒ _____ ⇒ _____ ⇒ _____

11+ Example question

An 11+ Word Ladder question may look something like this:

Q Change one letter at a time to make the first word into the final word. The two answers must be real words.

COPE (_____) (_____) FORT

Method — Change one letter at a time

1) Identify the letter that appears in both the first and last word, in the same position.

   C**O**PE (_____) (_____) F**O**RT ← The letter 'o' is the second letter in both words — this letter won't change.

2) Replace the first letter of 'cope' with the first letter of 'fort'. It doesn't make a new word, so replace the third letter of 'cope' with the third letter of 'fort' and so on, until you make a new word.

   FOPE ✗ FORT   CORE ✓ FORT

   Remember that you can't switch the letter positions around.

3) To find the third word, repeat the same method as before — replace the letters of 'core' with the letters from 'fort' until you make a new word.

   FORE ✓ FORT ← Remember, you don't have to change the second or third letters of 'core' because they already match the equivalent letters in 'fort'.

4) With the missing words in place, you should only have to change one letter to make the last word.

   COPE (_CORE_) (_FORE_) FORT ✓

Practice Questions

Change one letter at a time to make the first word into the final word. The two answers must be real words.

1) SPED (_____) (_____) FLEA   2) CASE (_____) (_____) BOSS

Section Two — Making Words

Section Three — Word Meanings

Preparing for the Test

Reading the dictionary isn't the only way to pass your VR test — read on for the lowdown...

Word Meanings Questions test your Vocabulary

Vocabulary means 'the set of words you know'. You can increase your vocabulary in a few ways:

1) Read lots of books and articles to help you learn new words.
2) Every time you come across a word you don't know, look it up in a dictionary and jot down the word and its definition in a notebook. Keep adding to the list and look over the words often.
3) Play word games such as SCRABBLE® or do crosswords to get you thinking about word meanings and how words are formed.
4) Do plenty of VR practice questions.

It's important to read lots of different types of books: fiction, non-fiction and poetry as well as newspaper articles.

Practise spotting different Word Types

1) 'Word type' means what category a word belongs to — e.g. noun, verb, adjective or adverb.
2) Here are a few tips to help you work out the word types:

Nouns are people, places or things

1) Concrete nouns are objects and things. They can have 'a', 'an', 'the' or 'some' in front of them. — a cow, an apple, the dog, some milk
2) Abstract nouns are harder to spot — they're things you can't see, hear, taste, touch or smell.
3) Abstract nouns can have 'my', 'his', 'her' or 'their' in front of them. — my childhood, his freedom, her bravery

Verbs describe actions

Some words belong to more than one word type. E.g. 'I catch fish', 'there's a catch'. 'Catch' is a verb in the first sentence and a noun in the other.

1) A verb is a doing word.
2) Verbs can go after 'I', 'you', 'he', 'it', 'she' or 'they'. — I play, you dance, they sing, it was

Adverbs describe verbs

Some adverbs can describe adjectives or other adverbs, e.g. "totally", "very", "quite".

Adverbs often end in -ly.

quickly, happily, playfully

Adjectives describe nouns

Adjectives sometimes end with -y, -ly, -ing.

sandy, friendly, interesting

Use Word Type to work out the Answer

Knowing and recognising word types can be a useful way of solving some questions in your VR test.

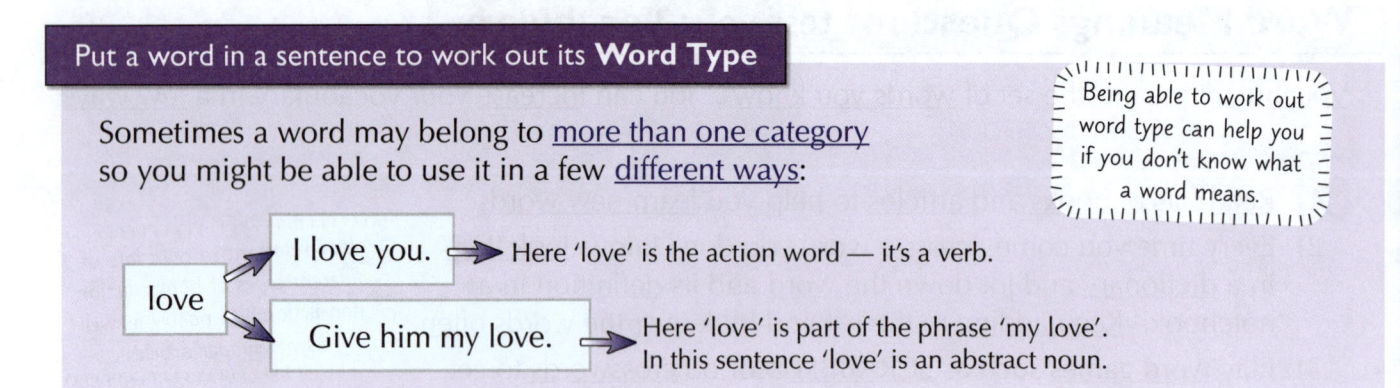

Put a word in a sentence to work out its Word Type

Sometimes a word may belong to more than one category so you might be able to use it in a few different ways:

love → I love you. → Here 'love' is the action word — it's a verb.

love → Give him my love. → Here 'love' is part of the phrase 'my love'. In this sentence 'love' is an abstract noun.

Being able to work out word type can help you if you don't know what a word means.

Look at word endings to help you work out Word Type

1) Sometimes you might need to find words that mean the same thing.
2) If you don't recognise some of the words, you could try looking at word type to help you.

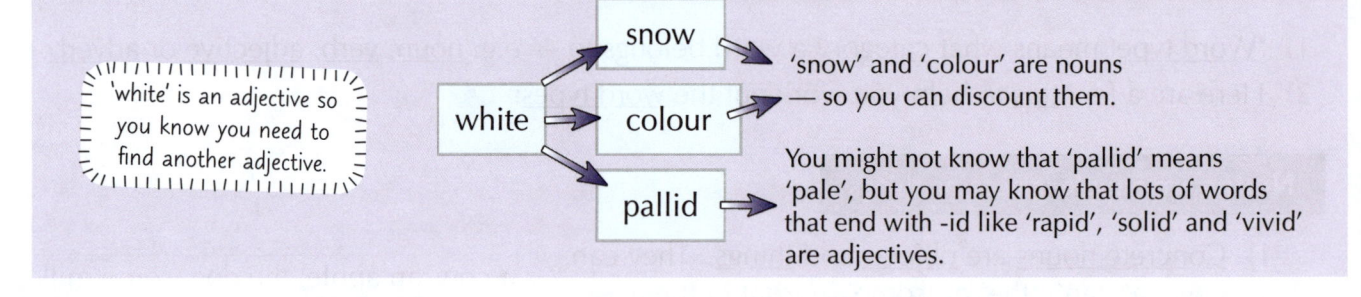

white → snow
white → colour
white → pallid

'white' is an adjective so you know you need to find another adjective.

'snow' and 'colour' are nouns — so you can discount them.

You might not know that 'pallid' means 'pale', but you may know that lots of words that end with -id like 'rapid', 'solid' and 'vivid' are adjectives.

Tips and Tricks

You'll recognise most of the words in your VR test — but occasionally they might sneak a tricky word in to test you. If you don't know it — don't worry. Try to eliminate any of the other possible answers, and if all else fails, make a sensible guess.

Practice Questions

1) Work out the word type of each of the following words:

a) sang b) honesty c) nosy d) tighten e) cryptic f) play g) vacantly

2) Work out the meaning and word type of the following words.

a) truth b) cantankerous c) wrathfully d) bemusement

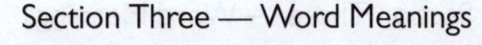

Check your answers in a dictionary.

Section Three — Word Meanings

Closest Meaning

This question type is about synonyms — that's another way of saying 'words with similar meanings'.

Warm-Up Activity

Some letters have been put in to start you off.

Find the synonyms and write the answers in the crossword.

DOWN
1) cheerful
2) shout
3) breezy

ACROSS
1) big
2) beautiful
3) unused
4) stop
5) friend

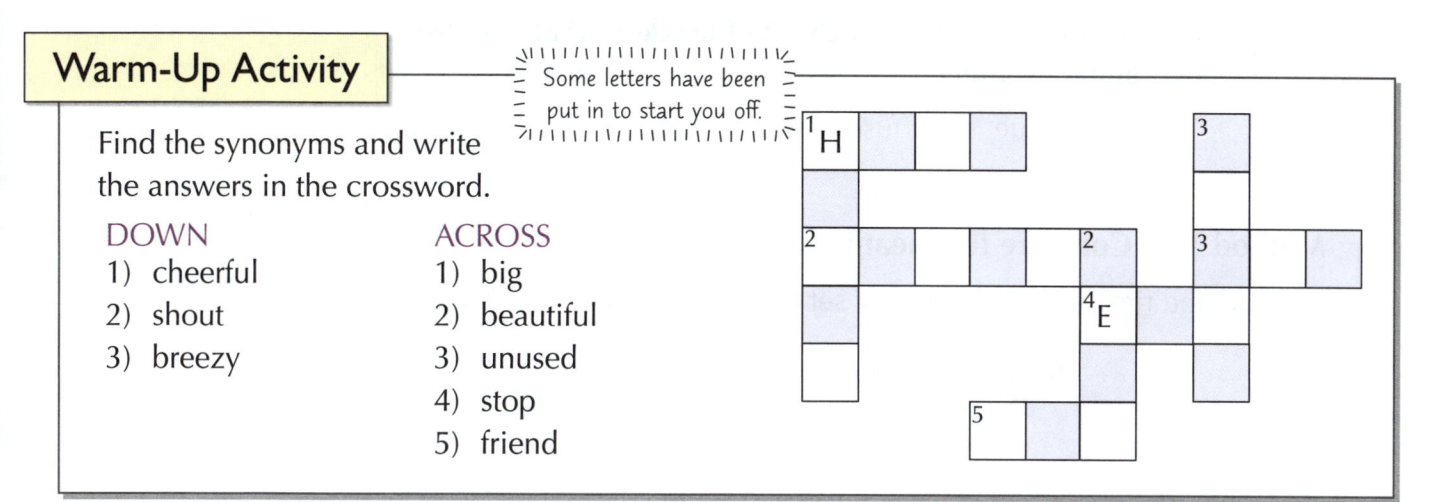

11+ Example Question

Here's an example of the sort of question you might get in the test:

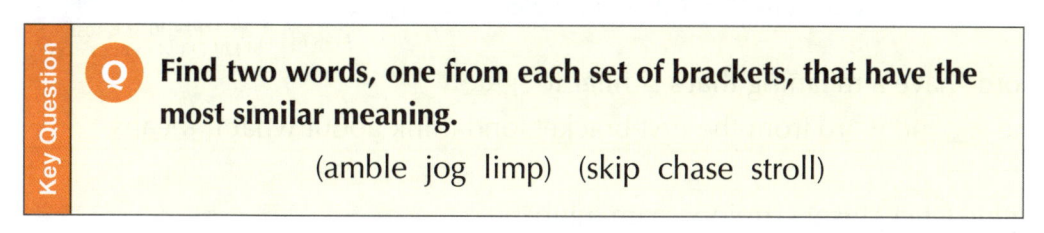

Q **Find two words, one from each set of brackets, that have the most similar meaning.**

(amble jog limp)   (skip chase stroll)

- You need to pick two words, one from each set of brackets, that have the closest meaning.
- So the answer to this question is 'amble' and 'stroll' — both these words mean 'to walk slowly'.

You need to know about Synonyms to answer these questions

1) Words with similar meanings are synonyms — e.g. small and tiny.
2) Pairs of synonyms are usually the same word type — e.g. nouns, verbs, adjectives or adverbs.

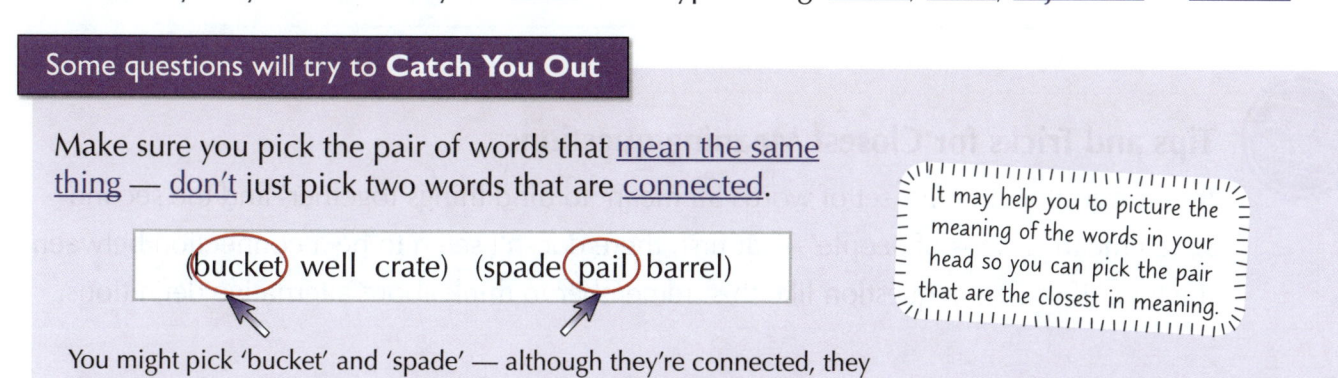

Some questions will try to Catch You Out

Make sure you pick the pair of words that mean the same thing — don't just pick two words that are connected.

It may help you to picture the meaning of the words in your head so you can pick the pair that are the closest in meaning.

(bucket well crate)   (spade pail barrel)

You might pick 'bucket' and 'spade' — although they're connected, they don't mean the same thing. The right answer is 'bucket' and 'pail'.

Section Three — Word Meanings

Use **Definitions** to help you answer the question

> **Q** Find two words, one from each set of brackets, that have the most similar meaning.
>
> (glue stick fuse) (union team club)

Method 1 — Compare the meanings of words

1) Take the first word from the first set of brackets and think about its meaning.

   (**glue** stick fuse) (union team club)

   'glue' means 'an adhesive' or 'to stick something together'.

2) Compare its meaning with each word in the second set of brackets.

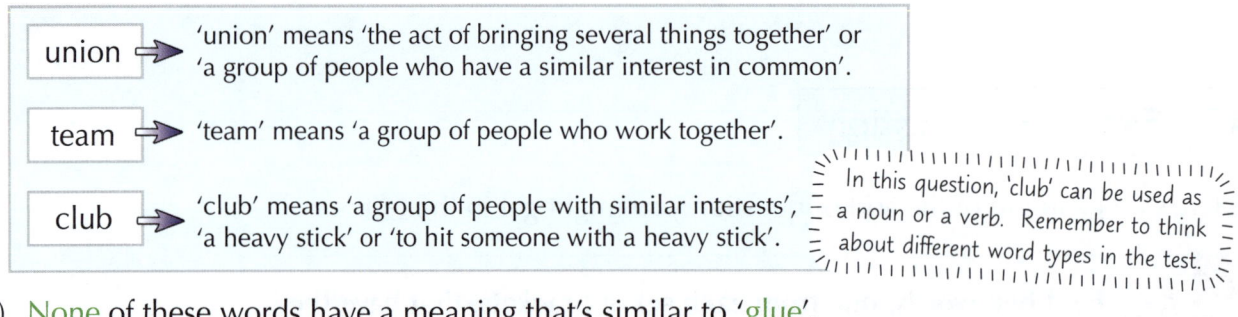

   union → 'union' means 'the act of bringing several things together' or 'a group of people who have a similar interest in common'.

   team → 'team' means 'a group of people who work together'.

   club → 'club' means 'a group of people with similar interests', 'a heavy stick' or 'to hit someone with a heavy stick'.

   In this question, 'club' can be used as a noun or a verb. Remember to think about different word types in the test.

3) None of these words have a meaning that's similar to 'glue'.

4) So move on to the second word from the first bracket, and think about what it means.

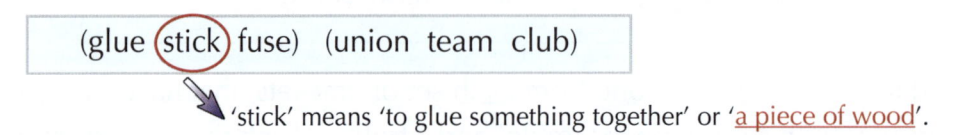

   (glue **stick** fuse) (union team club)

   'stick' means 'to glue something together' or 'a piece of wood'.

5) This definition is similar to something we've seen before...

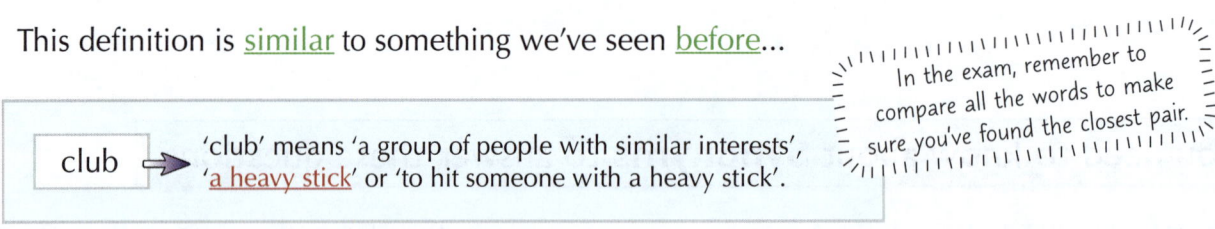

   In the exam, remember to compare all the words to make sure you've found the closest pair.

   club → 'club' means 'a group of people with similar interests', 'a heavy stick' or 'to hit someone with a heavy stick'.

6) 'stick' and 'club' are very close in meaning — so this is the answer.

TIPS & TRICKS

Tips and Tricks for Closest Meaning questions

In this question, the first set of words all mean 'to bind things together' and the second set all mean 'groups of people' — at first, there doesn't seem to be a connection between the two. If you get a question like this, remember to think about alternative definitions.

Section Three — Word Meanings

You can also look at **Word Type**

Key Question Q (chase rapidly competitive) (hasty immediate quickly)

Method 2 — Compare the word type

Take a look back at p.29 if you're not sure about word type.

1) The correct pair will often be the <u>same type of word</u> — two nouns, two verbs etc. — as well as having the <u>same meaning</u>.

2) Start by looking at <u>word meaning</u> and <u>rule out</u> any words that don't mean the same thing.

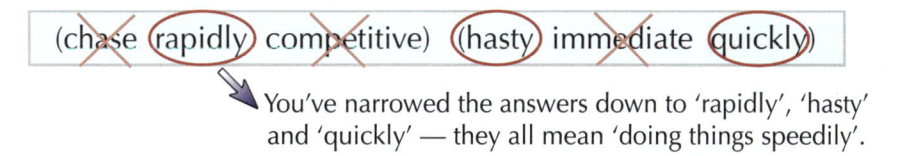

(chase ~~rapidly~~ competitive) (~~hasty~~ immediate ~~quickly~~)

You've narrowed the answers down to 'rapidly', 'hasty' and 'quickly' — they all mean 'doing things speedily'.

3) Take each word and <u>use it in a sentence</u> to help you work out the word type.

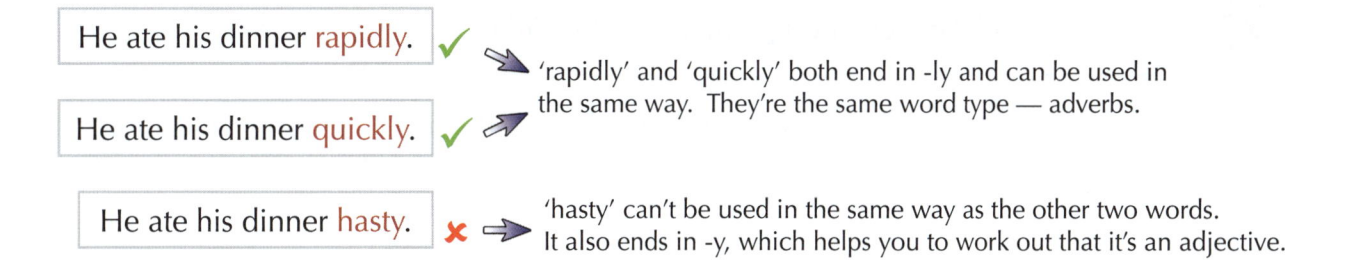

He ate his dinner **rapidly**. ✓
He ate his dinner **quickly**. ✓

'rapidly' and 'quickly' both end in -ly and can be used in the same way. They're the same word type — adverbs.

He ate his dinner **hasty**. ✗

'hasty' can't be used in the same way as the other two words. It also ends in -y, which helps you to work out that it's an adjective.

4) By looking at the <u>meaning</u> and the <u>word type</u>, you can work out that '<u>rapidly</u>' and '<u>quickly</u>' have the <u>closest meaning</u>.

Tips and Tricks

There's a similar question type that asks you to find words with the **most opposite** meanings (p. 34), so be sure to read the instructions carefully in the test and answer the right question.

Practice Questions

Find two words, one from each set of brackets, that have the most similar meaning.

1) (afraid scary menacing)   (aghast shocked terrified)
2) (stride traipse trail)   (rambler track tread)
3) (smiled laughed chuckled)   (grimaced happily beamed)

Section Three — Word Meanings

Opposite Meaning

The opposite of good is bad. The opposite of night is day. The opposite of synonym is antonym.

Warm-Up Activity

1) Look at the words below in red.
2) For each word, give yourself 30 seconds to write down as many words as you can which mean the opposite. Score one point for each correct answer.
3) Challenge a friend or parent to beat your score.

    happy   poor   serious   dainty

11+ Example Question

Here's an example of the sort of question you might get in the real thing:

> **Q** **Find two words, one from each set of brackets, that have the most opposite meaning.**
>
> (clean new fresh) (messy filthy dreary)

- Pick two words, one from each set of brackets that are the most different in meaning.
- The answer is 'clean' and 'filthy' because 'filthy' means 'dirty' which is the opposite of 'clean'.

This question is asking about Antonyms

1) Words that have the opposite meaning are antonyms — e.g. new and old.
2) Here are some more examples of antonyms:

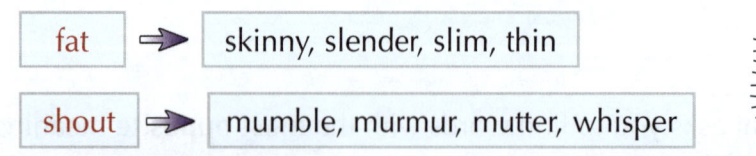

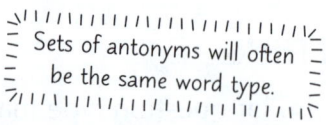

| fat | ⇒ | skinny, slender, slim, thin |
| shout | ⇒ | mumble, murmur, mutter, whisper |

Sets of antonyms will often be the same word type.

Look at the Prefixes

You can turn some words into antonyms by adding certain prefixes such as un-, dis- or in-.

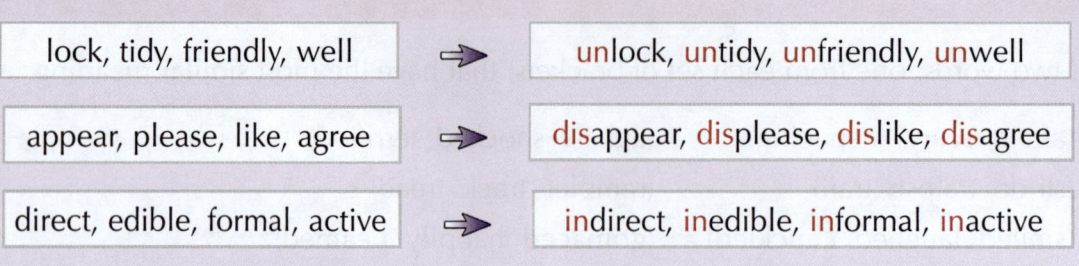

lock, tidy, friendly, well	⇒	unlock, untidy, unfriendly, unwell
appear, please, like, agree	⇒	disappear, displease, dislike, disagree
direct, edible, formal, active	⇒	indirect, inedible, informal, inactive

Section Three — Word Meanings

Use **Definitions** to help you answer the question

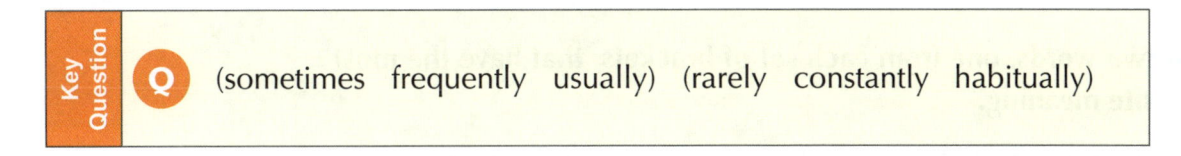

Key Question
Q (sometimes frequently usually) (rarely constantly habitually)

Method 1 — Compare the meanings of words

You can use a similar method for the opposite and closest meanings questions.

1) Take the first word from the first set of brackets and think about its meaning.

((sometimes) frequently usually) (rarely constantly habitually)
→ 'sometimes' means 'every now and then'.

2) Compare its meaning with each word in the second set of brackets.

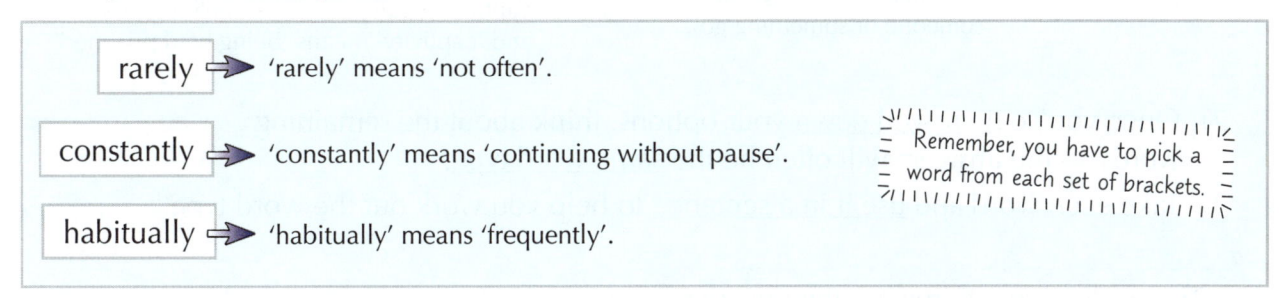

rarely ⇒ 'rarely' means 'not often'.
constantly ⇒ 'constantly' means 'continuing without pause'.
habitually ⇒ 'habitually' means 'frequently'.

Remember, you have to pick a word from each set of brackets.

3) None of these words have a meaning that's directly opposite to 'sometimes'.

4) So move on to the second word from the first bracket, and think about what it means.

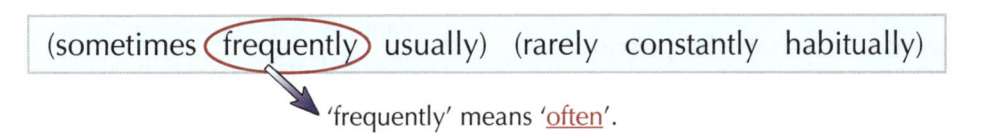

(sometimes (frequently) usually) (rarely constantly habitually)
→ 'frequently' means 'often'.

5) This definition means the opposite to something we've seen before...

rarely ⇒ 'rarely' means 'not often'.

In the exam, remember to compare all the words to make sure you've found the words with the most opposite meaning.

6) 'frequently' and 'rarely' are almost opposites — so that's your answer.

TIPS & TRICKS

Tips and Tricks for Opposite Meaning questions

Sometimes there might be another pair of words that seems like a possible answer, for example 'sometimes' and 'constantly'. The trick here is to think carefully about what each word means (trying both words in the same sentence may help you, e.g. "I swim sometimes" and "I swim constantly") and to pick the pair of words that are the **most opposite** in meaning.

Section Three — Word Meanings

Narrow Down the options and use Word Type to find the answer

Key Question

Q Find two words, one from each set of brackets, that have the most opposite meaning.

(enemy hostage release) (unlock capture captivity)

Method 2 — Compare the word type

1) Read the question. Think about the meanings of the words and rule out any words that don't have antonyms in the question.

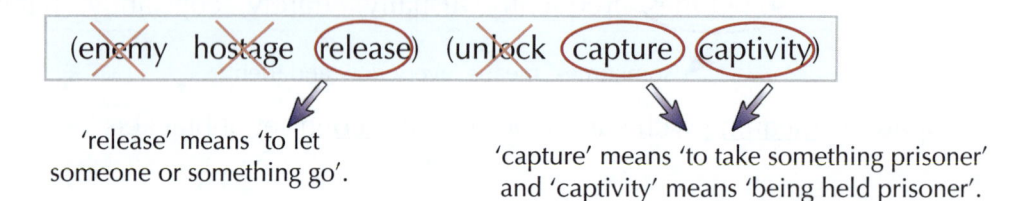

(e~~nemy~~ ho~~stage~~ (release)) (un~~lock~~ (capture) (captivity))

'release' means 'to let someone or something go'.

'capture' means 'to take something prisoner' and 'captivity' means 'being held prisoner'.

2) Once you've narrowed down your options, think about the remaining words — the answers will often be the same word type.

3) Take each word and use it in a sentence to help you work out the word type.

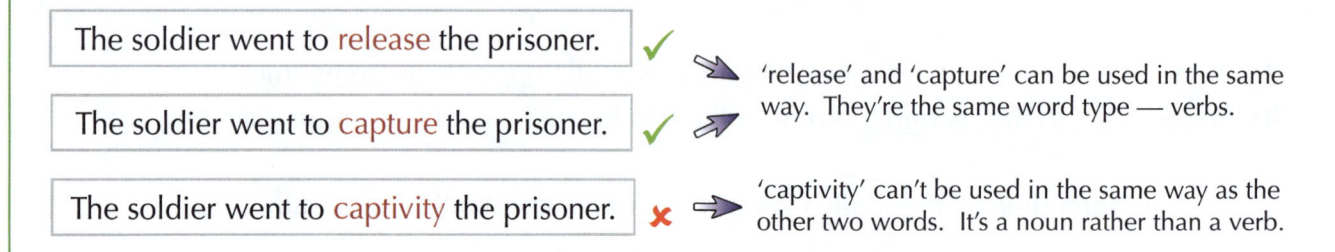

| The soldier went to release the prisoner. | ✓ |
| The soldier went to capture the prisoner. | ✓ |

'release' and 'capture' can be used in the same way. They're the same word type — verbs.

| The soldier went to captivity the prisoner. | ✗ |

'captivity' can't be used in the same way as the other two words. It's a noun rather than a verb.

4) By looking at the meaning and the word type, we can work out that 'release' and 'capture' are the most opposite in meaning.

Tips and Tricks for Opposite Meaning questions

Some words may belong to more than one word type, so you might need to try them in a couple of sentences to make sure you've got the right answer.

Practice Questions

Find two words, one from each set of brackets, that have the most opposite meaning.

1) (absent blank vacant)   (present available missing)
2) (claim accuse argue)   (protect guard defend)
3) (abolish hinder renounce) (endure establish extend)

Section Three — Word Meanings

Multiple Meanings

These questions are about homographs — that's 'a word with more than one meaning' to you and me.

Warm-Up Activity

1) Look at the words below.
2) For each word, write down two different meanings it may have.

    rich   ruler   match   fly   row

If you get stuck, use a dictionary to help you.

11+ Example Question

Take a look at this 11+ sample question:

> **Q** **Choose the word that has a similar meaning to the words in both sets of brackets.**
>
> (sphere globe) (dance party)   orb   spin   ball   gala   circle

- You need to pick one of the five options which has the same meaning as the words in brackets.
- So the answer is 'ball' because it can mean both 'a sphere or globe' and 'a dance or party'.

You need to be able to recognise Homographs for this question

Homographs have the Same Spelling

Homographs are words that have the same spelling but different meanings:

| My watch is an hour fast. | I watch TV after dinner. |

Homographs often belong to different word types.

The word 'watch' has two different meanings in these sentences.
You only know which meaning it is by reading the rest of the sentence.

Some homographs are Pronounced Differently

Some homographs have the same spelling, but are pronounced differently:

| A female pig is a sow. | The farmer was going to sow his seeds. |

The word 'sow' has two different meanings in these sentences.
They're also pronounced differently, but they're both spelt the same.

Section Three — Word Meanings

Work through each word **One By One**

Q **Choose the word that has a similar meaning to the words in both sets of brackets.**

(greet salute) (sleet snow)   wave   rain   bow   hail   storm

Method 1 — Rule out the wrong options

1) <u>Read</u> through the words in the <u>brackets</u>.
2) Think about what both sets <u>mean</u>.

You might not recognise one of the words in brackets, but the other one will mean the same thing. Work with the word you do know.

(greet salute) (sleet snow)   wave   rain   bow   hail   storm

'greet' and 'salute' mean 'to address someone'.

'sleet' and 'snow' are types of wet weather.

3) Take a look at the five options and try to <u>rule out</u> any possible answers.

~~wave~~   rain   ~~bow~~   hail   storm

'wave' and 'bow' can be a way of addressing someone, but they don't relate to wet weather — you can ignore them.

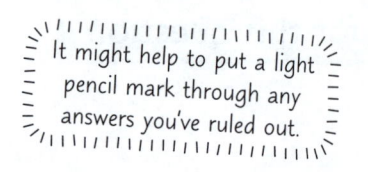

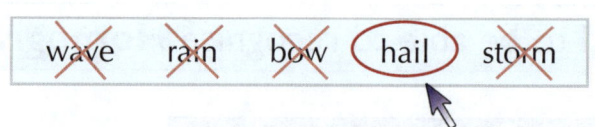

It might help to put a light pencil mark through any answers you've ruled out.

~~wave~~   ~~rain~~   ~~bow~~   (hail)   ~~storm~~

'rain' and 'storm' are types of wet weather, but they don't mean 'to address or salute'. That leaves us with 'hail'.

4) <u>Double check</u> your answer by using the word in <u>two sentences</u> — one for <u>each meaning</u>.

The weather forecast predicted hail. ✓   All hail the new king. ✓

TIPS & TRICKS

Tips and Tricks for Multiple Meanings questions

If you come across a word you don't know — don't panic! Rule out the answers that are definitely wrong, then if you've got more than one possible answer left, make a sensible guess.

Section Three — Word Meanings

Try putting the words into a **Sentence**

Key Question

Q (waft blow) (admirer devotee) supporter follower breeze fan gust

Method 2 — Use each word in a sentence

1) <u>Read</u> through the question. <u>Think</u> about what the words in the brackets <u>mean</u>.

'waft' and 'blow' both mean 'to move air'. → (waft blow) (admirer devotee) ← 'admirer' and 'devotee' mean someone who is enthusiastic about something.

2) Take the <u>first set</u> of brackets, and <u>rule out</u> any of the answers that don't <u>match</u> that <u>definition</u>.

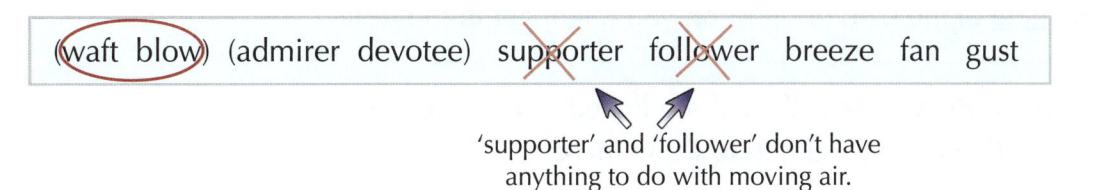

(waft blow) (admirer devotee) ~~supporter~~ ~~follower~~ breeze fan gust

'supporter' and 'follower' don't have anything to do with moving air.

3) Take the <u>second set</u> of brackets and use one of the words in a <u>sensible sentence</u>.

(admirer devotee) → I'm a devotee of Ulverston United football club.

4) Take <u>each</u> of the <u>remaining</u> possible answers and use them in the <u>same sentence</u>. There should only be <u>one word</u> that <u>makes sense</u> in the <u>same sentence</u> — and that's the <u>answer</u>.

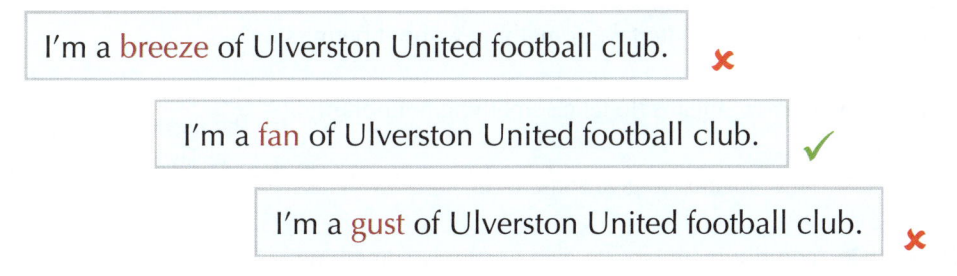

I'm a breeze of Ulverston United football club. ✗

I'm a fan of Ulverston United football club. ✓

I'm a gust of Ulverston United football club. ✗

5) The answer is '<u>fan</u>' because it matches the definitions for <u>both</u> sets of words.

Practice Questions

Choose the word that has a similar meaning to the words in both sets of brackets.

1) (lecture discussion) (chat natter) speak talk project articulate speech
2) (manage supervise) (sprint dash) boss jog rush run oversee
3) (schedule reserve) (novel text) story book organise arrange manual

Section Three — Word Meanings

Odd Ones Out

The best way to prepare for Odd Ones Out questions is to make sure your vocabulary is top-notch...

Warm-Up Activity

1) Ask your parent or guardian to give you a category.
2) Try to think of as many words as you can that belong in that category — score one point for each word.
3) See who can get the highest score in your family.

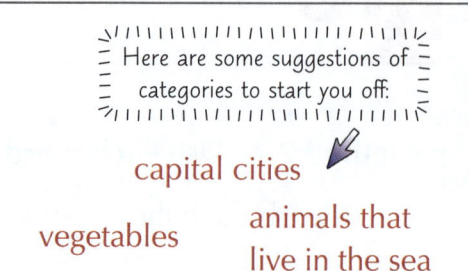

Here are some suggestions of categories to start you off:

capital cities

vegetables

animals that live in the sea

11+ Example Question

Here's an example of the kind of question you might get in the test:

Key Question

Q **Three of the words in the list are linked. Mark the two words that are not related to these three.**

steal   borrow   lend   contribute   snatch

- You need to pick two of the five words that aren't connected to the other three.

Method 1 — Compare the meanings of words

1) Read through all the words. Think about what each word means.

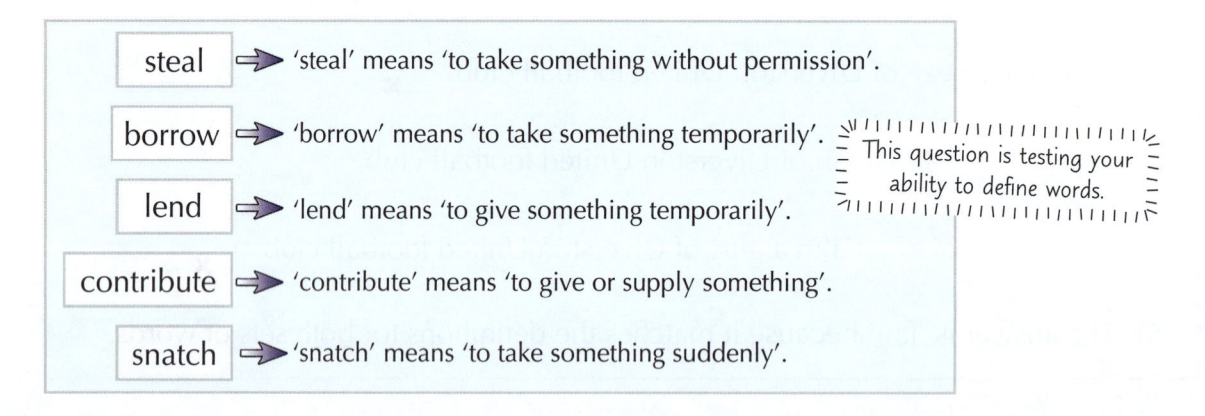

   steal ⇒ 'steal' means 'to take something without permission'.
   borrow ⇒ 'borrow' means 'to take something temporarily'.
   lend ⇒ 'lend' means 'to give something temporarily'.
   contribute ⇒ 'contribute' means 'to give or supply something'.
   snatch ⇒ 'snatch' means 'to take something suddenly'.

   This question is testing your ability to define words.

2) Try to make a connection between three of the words.

   The odd ones out won't always be connected to each other — they just have to be unrelated to the other three.

   ~~steal~~   ~~borrow~~   (lend)   (contribute)   ~~snatch~~

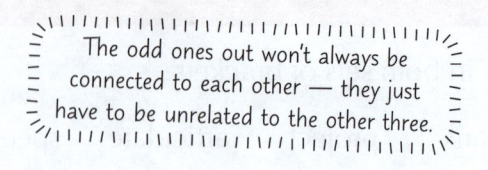

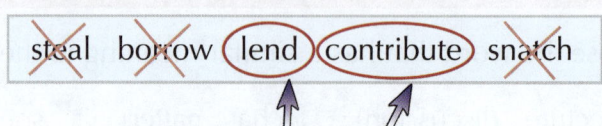

   'steal', 'borrow' and 'snatch' all mean 'to take'
   — 'lend' and 'contribute' mean 'to give'.

3) The odd ones out are 'lend' and 'contribute' — so that's your answer.

Section Three — Word Meanings

Use **Word Type** to find the answer

Key Question Q   blemish   error   wrongly   flaw   mark

Method 2 — Compare the word type

1) Sometimes you might get a list of words that have similar meanings. To solve these types of questions it might help to think about word type.

2) Read through all the words. Think about the word type of each word.

   blemish   error   wrongly   flaw   mark
   noun verb   noun   adverb   noun verb   noun verb

   Remember some words belong to more than one word type.

3) Identify any word types that don't match the others. So in this question, 'wrongly' is one half of the answer.

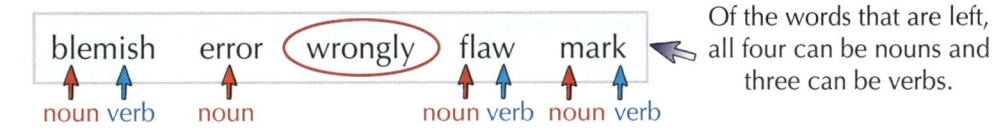

   blemish   error   (wrongly)   flaw   mark
   noun verb   noun   noun verb   noun verb

   Of the words that are left, all four can be nouns and three can be verbs.

4) Try and make a connection between three of the words.

   blemish   error   flaw

   'Blemish' and 'flaw' both mean 'an imperfection' or 'to make an imperfection'. 'Error' means 'something misguided or incorrect'.

   'Mark' can mean 'a score' or 'to give a score', but it can also mean 'an imperfection' or 'to make an imperfection'.

   ~~blemish~~   ~~flaw~~   ~~mark~~

5) 'Blemish', 'flaw' and 'mark' are synonyms, so 'wrongly' and 'error' are the odd ones out.

Tips and Tricks for Odd Ones Out questions

If you're given a group of five nouns the question will be testing your general knowledge.
It may help you to picture each of the objects in your head to help you spot the odd ones out.

Practice Questions

Three of the words in each list are linked. Mark the two words that are **not** related to these three.

1) calm   peaceful   dull   dreary   tedious
2) poem   biography   recipe   newspaper   novel
3) lethargic   drowsy   slumbering   listless   dormant

Section Three — Word Meanings

Word Connections

Word Connections questions look a bit complicated but they're less scary once you know the tricks...

Warm-Up Activity

Look at the chains of words below. For each chain, think how each word is linked to the next.
- car ➡ wheel ➡ bicycle ➡ helmet ➡ safety ➡ fireman ➡ hose
- dog ➡ bone ➡ skeleton ➡ scary ➡ spider ➡ web ➡ internet

11+ Example Question

Take a look at this 11+ style question — you might get something like this in the test:

> **Q** Choose two words, one from each set of brackets, that complete the sentence in the most sensible way.
>
> **Red** is to (pink   colour   paint) as **eight** is to (spider   age   number).

- You need to make a connection between one word from each set of brackets and the words in bold. Both pairs of words should be linked in the same way.
- So the answers are 'colour' and 'number' because red is a colour and eight is a number.

Words can be linked in Different Ways

Synonyms

The answers have the same definition as the words in the question.

> **Silly** is to (joke foolish clown) as **sensible** is to (teacher boring reasonable).

In this example, 'foolish' is a synonym of 'silly', and 'reasonable' is a synonym of 'sensible'.

Antonyms

The answers have the opposite meaning to the words in the question.

> **Calm** is to (ocean frenzied serene) as **happy** is to (sad family birthday).

Here, 'calm' is an antonym of 'frenzied', and 'happy' is an antonym of 'sad'.

Context

Sometimes the question might test your general knowledge.

> **Cue** is to (actor traffic snooker) as **racket** is to (noisy tennis sport).

To answer this question, you need to know that snooker players use cues and tennis players use rackets.

Section Three — Word Meanings

Think of **Links** between the words

Key Question

Q **Horse** is to (foal field bridle) as **swan** is to (bird feather cygnet).

Method 1 — Compare the meanings

1) Take the first word and think about its meaning.

   A horse is an animal that can be ridden, and that lives in fields or on farms. ← **Horse** is to (foal field bridle)

2) Take a look at the words in the first bracket and try and link them to 'horse'.

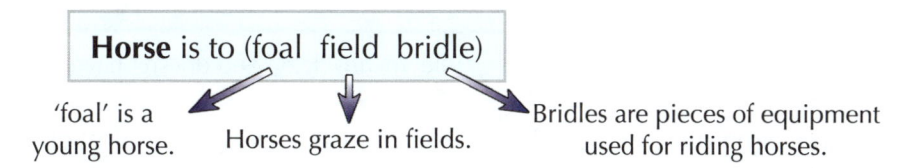

   Horse is to (foal field bridle)

   'foal' is a young horse.   Horses graze in fields.   Bridles are pieces of equipment used for riding horses.

3) Think about the meaning of the second word.

   A swan is a bird that lives in fresh water. ← **swan** is to (bird feather cygnet).

4) Look at the words in the second bracket. Think about what links them to 'swan'.

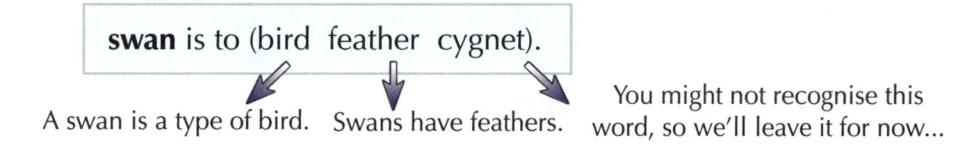

   swan is to (bird feather cygnet).

   A swan is a type of bird.   Swans have feathers.   You might not recognise this word, so we'll leave it for now...

5) Try to eliminate any words that definitely aren't right.

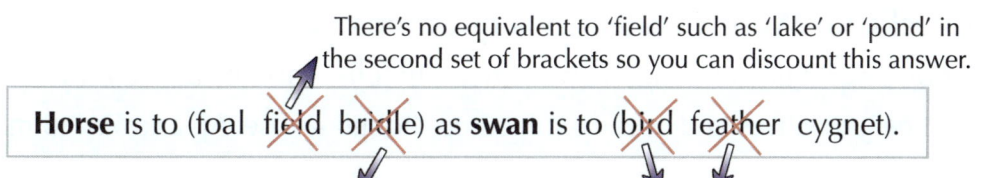

   There's no equivalent to 'field' such as 'lake' or 'pond' in the second set of brackets so you can discount this answer.

   Horse is to (foal f~~ield~~ br~~idle~~) as **swan** is to (b~~ird~~ fea~~ther~~ cygnet).

   You can't ride a swan, and there's no equivalent to 'bridle' in the second set of brackets.   If either of these were the answer you would expect the equivalents, like 'mammal' and 'fur', in the first set of brackets.

   Horse is to foal as **swan** is to cygnet. ✓

6) 'Cygnet' is the name given to a baby swan. This example shows that if you come across a word you don't know you shouldn't panic. Just work around it as much as you can.

Section Three — Word Meanings

Use **Word Types** to help you

> **Q** Choose two words, one from each set of brackets, that complete the sentence in the most sensible way.
>
> **Fearless** is to (soldier intrepid bravely) as **cowardly** is to (idle fled timid).

Method 2 — Compare the word type

1) If the words have similar meanings it might help to think about their word type.

2) Read the question. If you can, rule out any answers that don't have a connection.

> **Fearless** is to (soldier intrepid bravely) as **cowardly** is to (~~idle~~ fled timid).

'idle' means 'lazy' and doesn't have any connection to 'cowardly'.

3) Look at the remaining words. Try to work out the word type of each word.

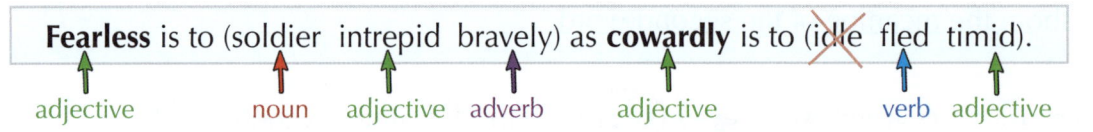

> **Fearless** is to (soldier intrepid bravely) as **cowardly** is to (~~idle~~ fled timid).
> adjective   noun   adjective   adverb   adjective   verb   adjective

4) Try to spot a link between the word types. In this example, both 'fearless' and 'cowardly' are adjectives, and there's a matching adjective in each of the brackets — 'intrepid' and 'timid'.

5) Double check your answer makes sense by reading it through.

> **Fearless** is to intrepid as **cowardly** is to timid. ✓

The answer won't always be the same word type as the question.

Tips and Tricks for Word Connections questions

In the test, don't waste time writing the word types in full — abbreviate verb to 'V' and noun to 'N'. Don't get adjectives and adverbs mixed up though — use 'Aj' and 'Av' to make it clear.

Practice Questions

Choose two words, one from each set of brackets, that complete the sentence in the most sensible way.

1) **Lobster** is to (red shell sea) as **dog** is to (spotty blanket coat).
2) **Cut** is to (sharp hairdresser scissors) as **magnify** is to (detective telescope big).
3) **Fortunate** is to (unlucky chance rich) as **hairy** is to (follicle genetic bald).

Section Three — Word Meanings

Reorder Words to Make a Sentence

Reorder the sentence in this words and halfway you're there...

Warm-Up Activity

1) Look at the sentences below.
2) For each sentence, fill in the gaps with sensible words so that each sentence makes sense.

- The farmer milked his _____ in the _____.
- I _____ my pizza while I _____ my book.
- Josephine has _____ hair and _____ eyes.

11+ Example question

Here's an example of the kind of question you might be asked in the test:

> **Q** Find the two words that should be swapped in order for this sentence to make sense.
>
> The burned microwave old my dinner.

- You need to swap a pair of words in the sentence so that it makes sense.

Method 1 — Identify the part that sounds wrong

1) Read through the sentence and identify the part that doesn't sound right.

   The burned microwave old my dinner.

   There's something funny going on here...

2) Once you've identified the bit that doesn't make sense, try switching a pair of words around.

   The microwave burned old my dinner.

   'burned' and 'microwave' have been swapped...   ...but this bit still doesn't sound right.

3) If your new sentence still doesn't sound right, go back to the original sentence and try switching another pair of words.

4) Once you're happy, check that the sentence sounds right.

   The old microwave burned my dinner. ✓

   This sounds more like it.

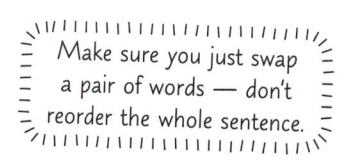

   Make sure you just swap a pair of words — don't reorder the whole sentence.

Section Three — Word Meanings

You can also look at Word Types

> **Q** Find the two words that should be swapped in order for this sentence to make sense.
>
> Jo girl the happiest is I know.

Method 2 — Compare the word type

1) <u>Read</u> the sentence. If you can't spot the words to swap <u>straight away</u>, read the sentence <u>again</u> and <u>identify</u> the part that doesn't <u>sound right</u>.

> Jo <u>girl the happiest is</u> I know.

2) This time, look at the <u>position</u> of different <u>word types</u> in the sentence.

> <u>Jo girl</u> the happiest <u>is</u> I <u>know</u>.

There are two nouns here.   There are two verbs here.

It looks like there are too many nouns at the start of the sentence and too many verbs at the end.

3) When you swap a pair of words, check that the <u>tenses match</u> and that they <u>agree</u>.

'Jo know' doesn't sound right — the verb and noun don't agree. It should be 'Jo knows'. → Jo <u>know</u> the happiest is I <u>girl</u>. ← The rest of the sentence sounds wrong too.

4) Swap the words until the sentence <u>makes sense</u> and it's <u>grammatically correct</u>.

The noun 'Jo' and the verb 'is' agree. → Jo <u>is</u> the happiest <u>girl</u> I know. ✓

TIPS & TRICKS

Tips and Tricks for Reorder Words to Make a Sentence questions

It'll really help you in the test if you're familiar with how sentences are constructed — reading lots of different books can help you get plenty of practice.

Practice Questions

Find the two words that should be swapped for each sentence to make sense.

1) Quickly the footpath if you want to get there take.
2) My Fluffy has a pet Beagle called Nan.
3) The bolts had silver robot and blue wires.
4) It's my birthday week a today.

Section Three — Word Meanings

Section Four — Maths and Sequences

Preparing for the Test

You just can't escape maths — it pops up everywhere, even in Verbal Reasoning...

Get used to doing maths Without a Calculator

1) You won't be allowed a calculator in your test, so you need to be able to do all the maths in your head or on paper.

2) Writing sums out on paper takes time — try and do as much as you can in your head. Here are some ideas to help you practise:

   - Do the maths-based puzzles in a puzzle magazine.
   - Play board games like YAHTZEE™, which test your maths skills.
   - Practise lots of different VR questions.

3) You'll have to work through sums with up to four steps, but these will only use addition, subtraction, multiplication and division:

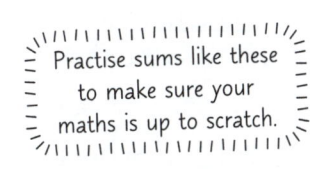

   | 8 + 4 = 12 | 8 − 4 = 4 | 8 × 4 = 32 | 8 ÷ 4 = 2 |

   Practise sums like these to make sure your maths is up to scratch.

Practise your Times Tables

1) Knowing your times tables will help you recognise factors and multiples, which are important in lots of the Maths and Sequences questions.

Factors

Factors are the numbers you can divide another number by to get a whole number.
The factors of 12 are:

| 12 ÷ **1** = 12 | 12 ÷ **2** = 6 | 12 ÷ **3** = 4 |
| 12 ÷ **4** = 3 | 12 ÷ **6** = 2 | 12 ÷ **12** = 1 |

So 12 has six factors: 1, 2, 3, 4, 6 and 12.

Multiples

Multiples are the numbers you get when you multiply a whole number by another whole number.
Some multiples of 3 are:

| 3 × 1 = **3** | 3 × 2 = **6** | 3 × 3 = **9** | 3 × 4 = **12** |
| 3 × 5 = **15** | 3 × 6 = **18** | 3 × 7 = **21** | 3 × 8 = **24** |

So any number in the three times table is a multiple of 3.

2) Practise with a friend by taking it in turns to test each other on your times tables. Test yourself by making times table flashcards with the answer on the back.

Think Logically for Sequence Questions

1) <u>Sequence</u> questions involve spotting <u>patterns</u> in the <u>jumps</u> between <u>numbers</u> or <u>letters</u>.
2) These jumps could be <u>alternating numbers</u>, <u>increasing</u> or <u>decreasing</u> numbers, <u>even</u> numbers etc.
3) You need to work out the <u>pattern</u> and think about what the <u>logical next step</u> would be.

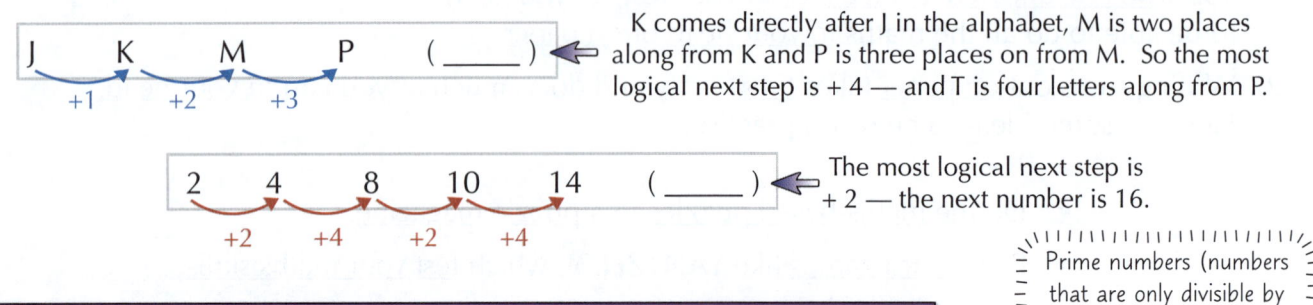

J K M P (____)
+1 +2 +3

K comes directly after J in the alphabet, M is two places along from K and P is three places on from M. So the most logical next step is + 4 — and T is four letters along from P.

2 4 8 10 14 (____)
 +2 +4 +2 +4

The most logical next step is + 2 — the next number is 16.

Prime numbers (numbers that are only divisible by themselves and 1) could come up too.

Sequences can be based on **Square numbers** or **Fibonacci numbers**

1) <u>Square numbers</u> are the numbers you get when you <u>multiply a number by itself</u>. Here are the first few:

   | 1 × 1 = **1** | 2 × 2 = **4** | 3 × 3 = **9** | 4 × 4 = **16** | 5 × 5 = **25** |

2) <u>Fibonacci sequences</u> are strings of numbers where <u>the two previous numbers</u> are <u>added together</u> to get the <u>next number</u> in the sequence. Here's an example:

   1 2 3 5 8 13

   The next number in the sequence would be 8 + 13 = **21**.

Learn the Alphabet to help you work Quickly

Make sure you <u>learn the alphabet</u> really well before the test. You'll often have to <u>count</u> along it or use it to find <u>patterns</u> in <u>Letter Sequences</u> questions.

The Alphabet Circle

1) For some Verbal Reasoning questions you'll need to <u>count backwards</u> from **A** to **Z** or <u>count on</u> from **Z** to **A**.
2) This is easier if you imagine the <u>alphabet</u> as a <u>continuous circle</u> — you can just keep <u>counting around the circle</u>.
3) For example, you can use it to find the <u>next letter</u> in this <u>sequence</u>:

   L O R U X (____)

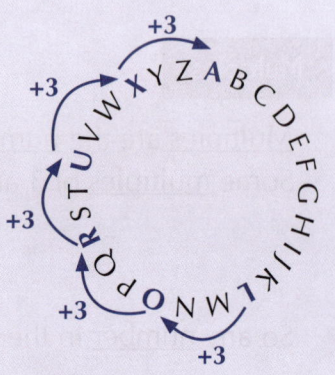

4) Use the <u>alphabet circle</u> to find the pattern — in this question you move <u>forward 3 letters each time</u>.
5) When you reach the <u>end</u> of the <u>alphabet</u>, use the <u>alphabet circle</u> to <u>continue counting</u>. This will help you work out that the <u>letter</u> after <u>X</u> is <u>A</u>.

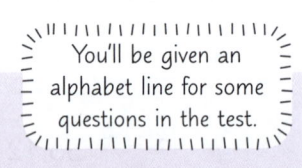

You'll be given an alphabet line for some questions in the test.

Section Four — Maths and Sequences

Complete the Sum

Don't be afraid of Complete the Sum questions — they're easier than they look.

Warm-Up Activity

Fill in the gaps to complete the sums.
The numbers in red are the answers.

Some numbers have been put in to start you off.

		6	×		+	2	=	**20**
		÷		×				×
20				8	÷		=	**2**
−		=		+				=
16	−		=	**2**				
=				=				
	×		+	12	=	**32**		

11+ Example Question

Here's an example of the sort of question you might get in the test:

Q **Find the missing number to complete the sum.**

$$15 \div 3 + 9 - 2 = (\_\_\_\_)$$

- You need to find the number that fills the gap so that the right hand side of the sum is equal to the left hand side.

Method 1 — Write the answer down as you go

1) Complete the Sum questions often have more than one step.
2) Look at the sum and work out the answer to the first step.

   $(15 \div 3) + 9 - 2 = (\_\_\_\_)$ ⟹ $15 \div 3 = 5$

3) Then use the answer in the second step.

   $5 + 9 = 14$

   Write down the answer to each step as you go along so you don't get confused.

4) Finally use that answer in the third step.

   $14 - 2 = 12$

5) This is the last step in the sum, so the answer to the sum is 12.

Tips and Tricks for Complete the Sum questions

Learn your times tables to help you answer these questions quickly in the real test.

Section Four — Maths and Sequences

Work on **One Half** of the sum at a time

Key Question

Q **Find the missing number to complete the sum.**

$24 \div 6 + 19 = 16 + (\_\_\_)$

Method 2 — Break the sum into two halves

1) Break the sum into two halves either side of the equals sign.

$24 \div 6 + 19 = 16 + (\_\_\_)$

$24 \div 6 + 19 = ?$ $? = 16 + (\_\_\_)$

2) Start with the sum which has all its numbers — this is usually the left hand sum.
3) Break the sum down into steps and do each step in order:

$24 \div 6 = 4$ ← This is where knowing your times tables is handy.

$4 + 19 = 23$ ← This next step is simple addition. Write it down if you need to.

4) Now you know that the answer to the left hand sum is 23.
5) The answer to the right hand sum has to equal the answer to the left hand sum. So you're looking for the number that will fill the gap and make the right hand sum equal to 23 too.

$23 = 16 + (\_\_\_)$

6) To fill in that last gap, you need to find the number that you can add to 16 to make 23. To do that, you need to subtract 16 from 23 to work out the difference between the two numbers.

$23 - 16 = 7$ ➡ $23 = 16 + (\underline{7})$ So the complete sum looks like this. ➡ $24 \div 6 + 19 = 16 + (\underline{7})$

TIPS & TRICKS

Tips and Tricks for Complete the Sum questions

Remember that the answer is the number that fills the gap in the sum, **not** the answer to both sums — make sure you mark the correct number in your test.

Practice Questions

Find the missing number to complete the sum.

1) $11 \times 4 = 24 + (\_\_\_)$
2) $30 - 4 = 19 + (\_\_\_)$
3) $54 \div 9 = 2 + (\_\_\_)$
4) $25 + 10 = 5 \times (\_\_\_)$
5) $3 \times 7 + 4 = 16 + (\_\_\_)$
6) $12 \div (\_\_\_) = 30 \div 6 - 2$
7) $15 \times 3 \div 5 = 27 - (\_\_\_)$
8) $18 \div 3 \times 2 + 4 = 10 + (\_\_\_)$

Section Four — Maths and Sequences

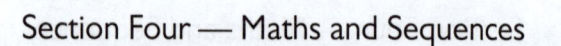

Letter Sequences

Letter Sequences can be tricky, but with a bit of practice they'll be a piece of cake.

Warm-Up Activity

1) Use paper and coloured pencils to make 26 cards with a letter of the alphabet on each card.
2) Mix them up, then challenge a friend to see who can lay them out in order the quickest.
3) Remove 3 letter cards, then spread out the remaining cards
   — see who can spot which ones are missing first.
4) Take out half the cards — try to put the remaining cards in alphabetical order.

11+ Example Question

You might be asked questions like this one in the test:

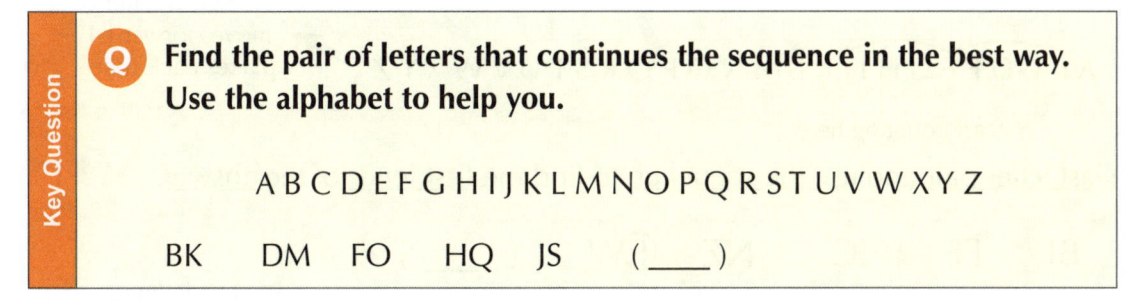

> **Q** **Find the pair of letters that continues the sequence in the best way. Use the alphabet to help you.**
>
> A B C D E F G H I J K L M N O P Q R S T U V W X Y Z
>
> BK   DM   FO   HQ   JS   (____)

- The pairs of letters are following a sequence based on their position in the alphabet.
- You have to work out what sequence they are following and then fill in the next letter pair.
- In this question both letters move forward two places in the alphabet each time. This means the next letter pair is LU.

The letters can move Independently

The letters don't always move the same number of steps or in the same direction, e.g.:

FY   HU   JQ   LM   (____)

The first letter moves forward 2 each time and the second letter moves back 4 each time.

A B C D E F G H I J K L M N O P Q R S T U V W X Y Z

The answer here is NI.

The Sequence can go Over the End of the Alphabet

Sometimes the sequence will move forwards past Z or backwards past A.
If this happens, just keep counting around to the other end of the alphabet.

H   F   D   B   (____)

A B C D E F G H I J K L M N O P Q R S T U V W X Y Z

The answer here is Z.

The alphabet circle on page 48 will help you practise this.

Section Four — Maths and Sequences

Use the **Alphabet** to **Count Out** the **Sequence**

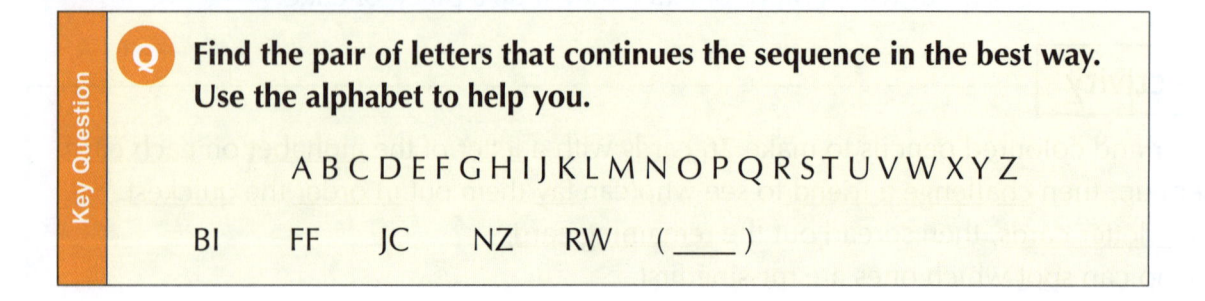

Key Question

Q Find the pair of letters that continues the sequence in the best way. Use the alphabet to help you.

A B C D E F G H I J K L M N O P Q R S T U V W X Y Z

BI   FF   JC   NZ   RW   (____)

Method 1 — Look at the first three pairs

1) Find the <u>first letter</u> of the <u>first pair</u> in the <u>alphabet</u>. Then <u>count the steps</u> to the <u>first letter</u> of the <u>second pair</u>. Do the same for the <u>second</u> and <u>third</u> pairs.

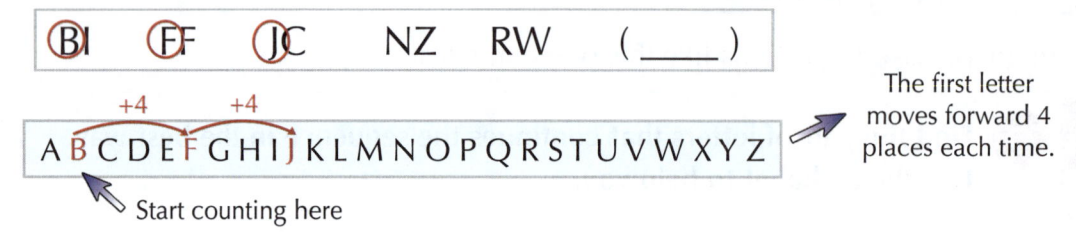

   (B)I   (F)F   (J)C   NZ   RW   (____)

   A B C D E F G H I J K L M N O P Q R S T U V W X Y Z
         +4   +4
   Start counting here

   The first letter moves forward 4 places each time.

2) Look at the <u>last letter pair</u> and <u>use the sequence</u> to find the <u>first letter</u> of the <u>answer</u>.

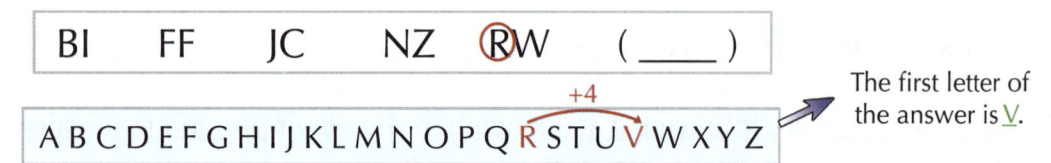

   BI   FF   JC   NZ   (R)W   (____)

   A B C D E F G H I J K L M N O P Q R S T U V W X Y Z
                                    +4

   The first letter of the answer is <u>V</u>.

3) Now find the <u>second letter</u> of the <u>first pair</u> in the <u>alphabet</u>. Count the steps to the <u>second letter</u> of the <u>second pair</u>, and then to the <u>second letter</u> of the <u>third pair</u>.

   A B C D E F G H I J K L M N O P Q R S T U V W X Y Z
       −3 −3

   The second letter moves back 3 places each time.

4) <u>Use the sequence</u> to count back from the last letter pair to find the <u>second letter</u> of the <u>answer</u>.

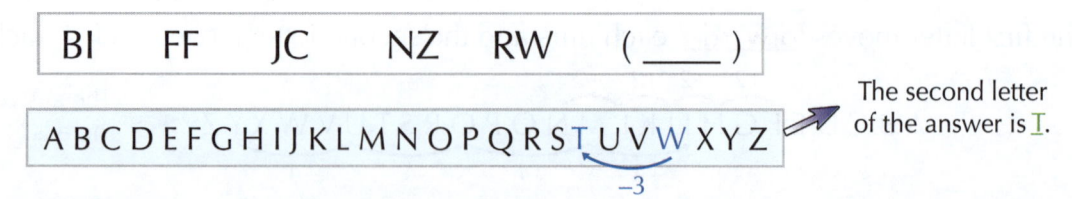

   BI   FF   JC   NZ   RW   (____)

   A B C D E F G H I J K L M N O P Q R S T U V W X Y Z
                               −3

   The second letter of the answer is <u>T</u>.

5) The <u>first letter</u> of the pair is <u>V</u> and the <u>second letter</u> is <u>T</u>, so the answer is <u>VT</u>.

Tips and Tricks for Letter Sequences questions

TIPS & TRICKS

Method 1 will save time in the test because you only have to look at the first three pairs. If the sequence is more complicated you'll need to look at all the pairs to find the correct answer (see Method 2).

Section Four — Maths and Sequences

Some **Questions** have more **Complex Sequences**

Key Question Q BS   CQ   EP   HN   LM   (____)

Method 2 — Look at the whole sequence

1) Use this method for tricky sequences, where the size of the gap between the pairs changes.
2) Start by looking at the first letter in the first three pairs.

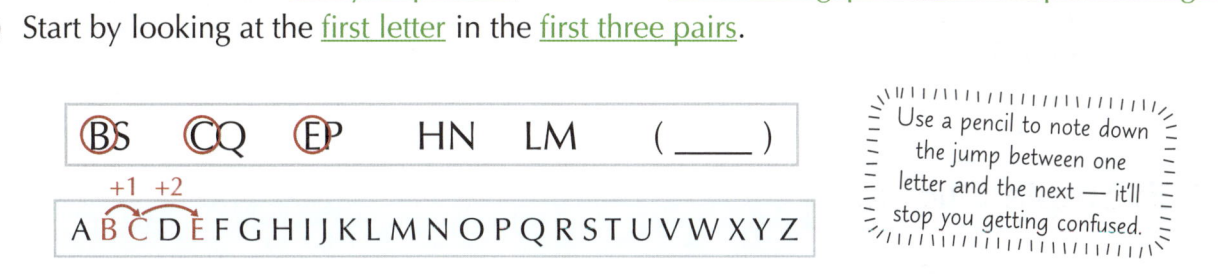

BS   CQ   EP   HN   LM   (____)
+1 +2
A B C D E F G H I J K L M N O P Q R S T U V W X Y Z

Use a pencil to note down the jump between one letter and the next — it'll stop you getting confused.

3) The jumps between the letters are different sizes, so you need to look at all the letter pairs.

+1 +2 +3 +4 +5
A B C D E F G H I J K L M N O P Q R S T U V W X Y Z

The jump between each letter increases by 1 each time, so the next letter in the sequence will be 5 letters on from L. → The first missing letter is Q.

4) Now look at the second letter in the first three pairs.

A B C D E F G H I J K L M N O P Q R S T U V W X Y Z
−1 −2

→ The jumps are different so you need to look at all of the pairs to establish the sequence.

A B C D E F G H I J K L M N O P Q R S T U V W X Y Z
−2 −1 −2 −1 −2

→ The jump alternates between moving back 1 place and back 2 places. The next step is back 2 places.

K is next in the sequence.

5) The first letter is Q and the second letter is K, so the answer is QK.

Practice Questions

Find the pair of letters that continues the sequence in the best way.
Use the alphabet at the top of the page to help you.

1) KP   MR   OT   QV   SX   (____)
2) FS   KO   PK   UG   ZC   (____)
3) BX   CB   FF   GJ   JN   (____)
4) NE   OG   OK   NM   LQ   (____)

Section Four — Maths and Sequences

Number Sequences

These pages on Number Sequences will make this question type as easy as 1, 2, 3...

Warm-Up Activity

1) Look at the <u>numbers</u> below.
2) On a piece of paper, sort the numbers into categories according to whether they belong to:
   a) the 7 times table
   b) the 3 times table
   c) the 5 times table

   40   12   18   21
   84   49   20
   15   35   56   28

   Some of the numbers belong to more than one times table.

11+ Example Question

Here's an <u>example</u> question for you to look at:

Key Question

Q **Find the number that continues the sequence in the best way.**

   48   41   34   27   (___)

- You need to work out the <u>rule</u> for the <u>number sequence</u> and use it to <u>fill in</u> the <u>missing number</u>.
- In this example the rule is to <u>subtract 7</u> each time, so the <u>answer</u> is <u>20</u>.

The Sequences follow Different Patterns

Sequences use Addition, Subtraction, Multiplication and Division

1) Simple sequences <u>add</u> or <u>subtract</u> the <u>same number</u> each time, e.g.:

   27   23   19   15   11   (_7_)   ⇐ The next number is 7.
     −4   −4   −4   −4   −4

2) Other sequences will <u>add</u> or <u>subtract increasing</u> or <u>decreasing</u> numbers, e.g.:

   Some sequences involve adding <u>and</u> subtracting.

   30   29   29   30   32   (_35_)   ⇐ The next number is 35.
     −1   0   +1   +2   +3

3) In some sequences the <u>previous two numbers</u> are added together to get the <u>next number</u> e.g.:

   2   4   6   10   16   (_26_)   ⇐ The next number is 26.
         2+4 4+6 6+10 10+16

4) Some sequences use <u>multiplication</u> or <u>division</u>, e.g.:

   2   4   8   16   (_32_)   ⇐ The next number is 32.
     ×2 ×2 ×2 ×2

Section Four — Maths and Sequences

Look at the **Differences** between the **Numbers**

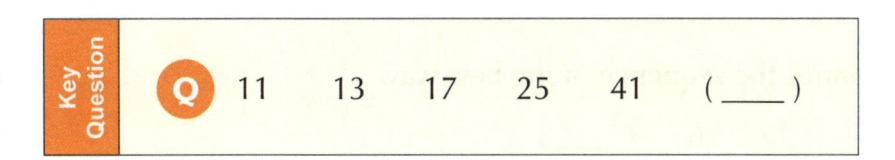

Key Question

Q 11   13   17   25   41   (____)

Method 1 — Work out the difference between each number

1) Look at the sequence. Work out the difference between each of the numbers by subtracting the smaller one from the larger one.

   11   13   17   25   41   (____)
      +2   +4   +8   +16

2) There is a pattern in the differences between the numbers — the jump doubles each time.

3) Use this pattern to work out what the next step will be. To find the next number in the sequence, you need to double 16 and add the result to the last number.

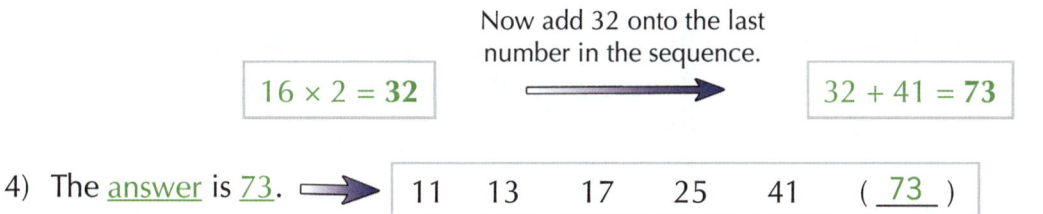

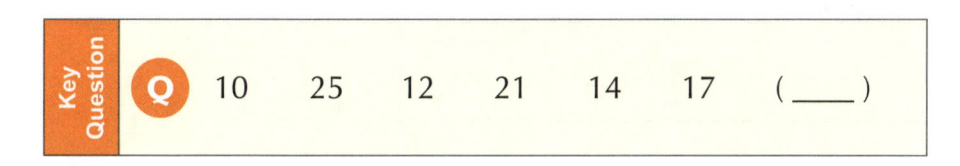

   Now add 32 onto the last number in the sequence.

   16 × 2 = **32**   ⟶   32 + 41 = **73**

4) The answer is 73. ⟹ 11   13   17   25   41   (_73_)

Key Question

Q 10   25   12   21   14   17   (____)

Method 2 — Work out the difference between alternate numbers

1) Look at the sequence — if there are more than five numbers, and they increase and decrease, it's probably an alternating sequence.

2) Look at the differences between alternate numbers, starting from the end of the sequence.

   – 2   – 2   ?
   10   25   12   21   14   17   (____)

   You only need to look at the sequence that leads to the answer — you can ignore the other sequence.

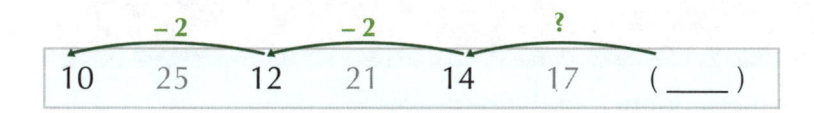

3) So the answer is 16 because if you take away 2 from 16, it gives you 14 — the previous number in the sequence.

Section Four — Maths and Sequences

Look for a **Relationship** between the **Numbers**

Key Question

Q Find the number that continues the sequence in the best way.

96   48   24   12   6   (___)

Method 3 — Look for multiplication or division

1) Look at the sequence to see if any of the numbers are factors or multiples of each other — sequences that contain factors and multiples usually use multiplication or division.

2) Start by looking at the smaller numbers — it's easier to see any relationship between them than the larger numbers. In this example you can see that 12 has been divided by 2 to get 6.

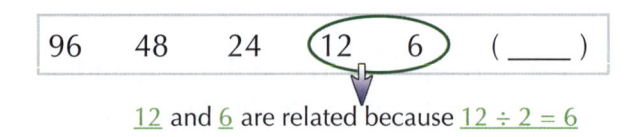

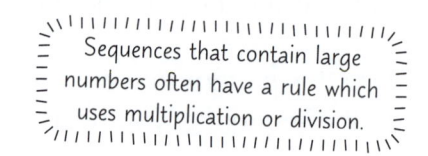

96   48   24   (12   6)   (___)

12 and 6 are related because 12 ÷ 2 = 6

Sequences that contain large numbers often have a rule which uses multiplication or division.

3) Once you've worked out how two of the numbers are related, you need to check whether your rule applies to the other numbers in the sequence. If the rule is to divide by 2 each time then you'd expect:

24 ÷ 2 = 12   and   48 ÷ 2 = 24   and   96 ÷ 2 = 48   ← These sums are correct so the rule must be to divide by 2.

4) Now that you're sure of the rule you need to work out the missing number in the sequence.

6 ÷ 2 = 3   →   96   48   24   12   6   (_3_)

The final answer is 3.

Tips and Tricks for Number Sequences questions

You'll be able to work faster in the test if you can do most of these sums in your head, but don't worry if you have to write some of them down — it's just as important to be accurate.

Practice Questions

Find the number that continues the sequence in the best way.

1) 52   48   43   39   (___)
2) 15   19   25   33   (___)
3) 37   26   19   14   (___)
4) 243   81   27   9   (___)

Section Four — Maths and Sequences

Related Numbers

These questions can be really sneaky, so read these pages carefully and be prepared.

Warm-Up Activity

1) Look at the numbers in the box.
2) Use the numbers in red in any combination, as many times as you like, to make the numbers in bold.
3) You can use any of the mathematical symbols — +, −, ÷ or × and as many of the red numbers as you like.
4) See how many different sums you can make.

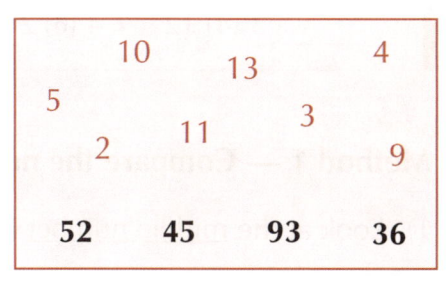

```
       10           4
    5      13
              3
       2  11        9

    52    45    93    36
```

11+ Example Question

Take a look at this 11+ sample question:

> **Q** **Find the number that completes the final set of numbers in the same way as the first two sets.**
>
> 10 (12) 22   9 (8) 17   4 (___) 15

- In each set the first and third number are used in a sum to make the middle number. You need to work out how the middle numbers are made, then fill in the missing number in the third set.
- In this question, the first number is subtracted from the third number to give the middle number. So the answer is 15 − 4 = 11.

Look at the Numbers in the First Two Sets

1) If the middle number is larger than the first and third numbers the sum probably uses multiplication or addition.

   2 (8) 4   3 (15) 5   4 (_12_) 3 → Multiply the first and third numbers to get the middle number.

2) If the middle number is smaller than or between the numbers either side, the sum probably uses subtraction or division.

   19 (14) 5   8 (5) 3   21 (_19_) 2 → Subtract the third number from the first number to get the middle number.

3) If the numbers are factors or multiples of each other, the sum probably uses division or multiplication.

   15 (5) 3   21 (3) 7   16 (_4_) 4 → Divide the first number by the third number to get the middle number.

4) Sometimes the middle number will be exactly halfway between the outer numbers.

   12 (10) 8   21 (11) 1   18 (_14_) 10 → The middle number is exactly halfway between the outer numbers.

Section Four — Maths and Sequences

Compare the Middle Number to the Outer Numbers

Key Question

Q Find the number that completes the final set of numbers in the same way as the first two sets.

3 (4) 12   4 (6) 24   6 (____) 30

Method 1 — Compare the numbers

1) Look at the middle number in the first two sets and compare it to the numbers on either side.

   3 (4) 12   4 (6) 24   6 (____) 30

   These numbers both lie between the two numbers outside the brackets, so the rule will probably use subtraction or division.

2) Try subtracting and dividing the outer numbers to see which one will give the middle numbers. Always divide the larger number by the smaller number and subtract the smaller number from the larger number.

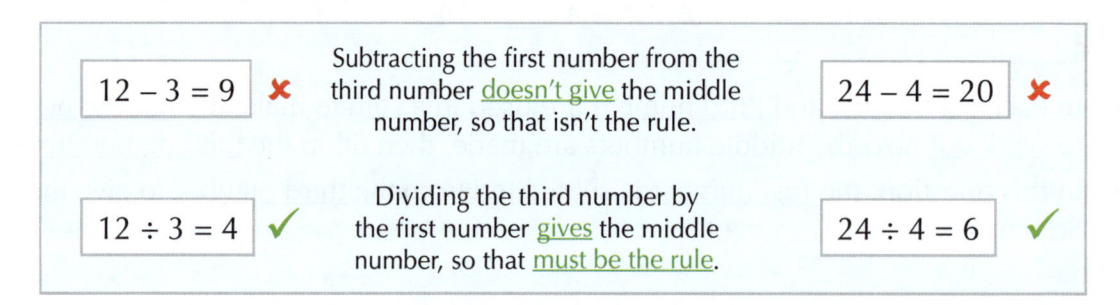

   12 − 3 = 9   ✗   Subtracting the first number from the third number doesn't give the middle number, so that isn't the rule.   24 − 4 = 20   ✗

   12 ÷ 3 = 4   ✓   Dividing the third number by the first number gives the middle number, so that must be the rule.   24 ÷ 4 = 6   ✓

3) The rule fits with both the first and second number sets. Now you can use it to find the missing number from the last set.

   30 ÷ 6 = 5 ⟶ 3 (4) 12   4 (6) 24   6 (5) 30

   The answer will always be a whole number — if you don't get one then go back and check your working.

TIPS & TRICKS

Tips and Tricks for Related Numbers questions

Look at the first two sets to help you work out whether the missing number will be bigger than, smaller than, or in-between the outer numbers in the final set. If you're doing a multiple-choice test, this might help you rule out some of the wrong answers.

Section Four — Maths and Sequences

More **Difficult Questions** use **Rules** with **More than One Step**

Q 11 (10) 6   14 (6) 11   19 (____) 8

Method 2 — Step by step calculation

1) Look at the outer numbers in each set first — the first step will normally use both numbers.

   (11)(10)(6)   (14)(6)(11)   19 (____) 8

2) The outer numbers aren't factors or multiples of each other, so the sum probably doesn't use multiplication or division first. It probably uses addition or subtraction — you'll need to try both.

   There's more on factors and multiples on page 47.

3) Add the outer numbers in each set and see if the answer is connected to the middle number.

   Compare the answers with the middle number from each set.

   11 + 6 = 17   and   14 + 11 = 25

   10 and 17   No obvious connections.   6 and 25

4) Adding the outer numbers doesn't reveal any obvious link to the middle number, so try subtracting the outer numbers.

   Compare the answers with the middle number from each set.

   11 − 6 = 5   and   14 − 11 = 3

   10 and 5   6 and 3

   For both sets you can multiply the answer by 2 to get the middle number.

5) So the rule is to subtract the third number from the first and then double the answer. Now use the rule with the numbers from the third set to get the missing number:

   19 − 8 = 11 ⇒ 11 × 2 = 22

6) The answer is 22.

Practice Questions

Find the number that completes the final set of numbers in the same way as the first two sets.

1) 17 (21) 4   9 (24) 15   31 (____) 7
2) 9 (17) 2   4 (23) 6   8 (____) 4
3) 5 (6) 15   7 (10) 35   4 (____) 16
4) 15 (22) 29   8 (12) 16   17 (____) 27

Section Four — Maths and Sequences

Letter-Coded Sums

Letter-Coded Sums are just sums where the numbers have been swapped for letters.

Warm-Up Activity

1) Look at the code below in red.
2) Use the letters to write as many sums as you can that give the answer 10.
3) You can subtract, add, multiply or divide and use as many letters as you like, as many times as you like in each sum.
4) Challenge a friend to see who can write the most sums.

A = 1   B = 2   C = 3   D = 4   E = 5

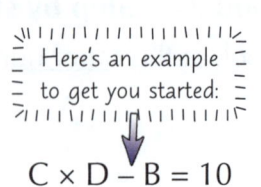

Here's an example to get you started:

C × D − B = 10

11+ Example Question

Here's an example of the kind of question you might get on the test:

Key Question

Q Each letter stands for a number. Work out the answer to the sum as a letter.
A = 2   B = 3   C = 5   D = 9   E = 11   D ÷ B + A = (___)

- Use the code to work out the answer to the sum using numbers. Then change the answer into a letter.
- The answer is C because 9 ÷ 3 + 2 = 5, and C is the code for 5.

Work through the sum Step by Step

1) Letter-Coded Sums often have calculations with 2 or 3 steps.
2) When you're working through a calculation you need to work out the answer to each step and then use that answer in the next step of the sum, e.g.:

A = 2   B = 3   C = 6   D = 16   E = 18   C × B − A = (___)

First step: C × B ⇒ 6 × 3 ⇒ 18   Second step: 18 − A ⇒ 18 − 2 ⇒ 16

Now convert 16 to a letter.

16 = D ⇒ D is the code for 16, so D is the answer you write down.

TIPS & TRICKS

Tips and Tricks for Letter-Coded Sums questions

Letter-Coded Sums questions involve multiplication and division, so learn your times tables to help you to answer these questions quickly in the test.

Section Four — Maths and Sequences

Change the Letters into Numbers

Key Question

Q) A = 3   B = 4   C = 8   D = 12   E = 18   D × B ÷ C + D = (____)

Method — Decode the sum

1) Look at the sum. Use the code in the question to change each letter into a number.

D × B ÷ C + D = (____) → 12 × 4 ÷ 8 + 12 = (____)
↑   ↑   ↑   ↑
12 4   8   12

2) Work through the sum step by step in order.

12 × 4 = **48** → 48 ÷ 8 = **6** → 6 + 12 = **18**

3) You need to write your answer as a letter, not a number.
   Look back at the code in the question to see which letter is used for 18.

A = 3   B = 4   C = 8   D = 12   (E = 18)

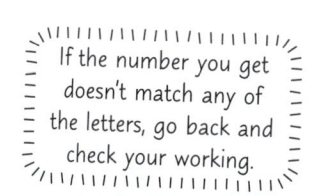

If the number you get doesn't match any of the letters, go back and check your working.

4) 18 is equal to E in the code, so the answer is E.

TIPS & TRICKS

Tips and Tricks for Letter-Coded Sums questions

Even if you can work out the sums in your head it's a good idea to write down the answer you get at each step of the calculation — it'll stop you getting confused.

Practice Questions

Each letter stands for a number. Work out the answer to the sum as a letter.

1) A = 2   B = 4   C = 7   D = 21   E = 28   C × B = (____)

2) A = 3   B = 7   C = 11   D = 14   E = 19   C × A − D = (____)

3) A = 3   B = 6   C = 9   D = 15   E = 45   E ÷ C × A = (____)

4) A = 4   B = 12   C = 17   D = 21   E = 27   B × A − C − E = (____)

Section Four — Maths and Sequences

Section Five — Logic and Coding

Preparing for the Test

Verbal Reasoning tests more than your vocab and maths skills — you also need to think logically.

You need to be Accurate to do well in Coding Questions

Coding questions test a range of skills:
1) Using the alphabet and counting accurately along it.
2) Spotting patterns and working out the next step.
3) Using logic to solve problems quickly.

Doing lots of practice will make Coding Questions easier

1) Do number and alphabet puzzles in puzzle books or on the internet.
2) Practise counting along the alphabet — use the alphabet circle on page 48 to help you practise counting backwards from A or forwards from Z.
3) Practise spotting letter pairs that are an equal distance from the centre of the alphabet. For example, the letters E and V are five letters in from each end of the alphabet, or nine letters out from the centre of the alphabet.

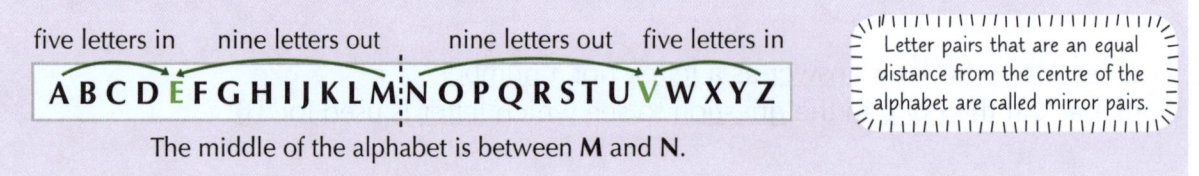

five letters in   nine letters out   nine letters out   five letters in
A B C D E F G H I J K L M : N O P Q R S T U V W X Y Z

The middle of the alphabet is between M and N.

Letter pairs that are an equal distance from the centre of the alphabet are called mirror pairs.

Logic Questions use lots of different skills

To do well in logic questions you need to be able to:
1) Read and understand information and pay attention to details.
2) Pick out key pieces of information to solve a problem, and ignore the bits that are irrelevant.
3) Do simple maths quickly.

You can Practise Logical Thinking in different ways

1) Buy a puzzle magazine — these often have puzzles just like Solve the Riddle (p. 72-74) and Word Grids (p. 75-76). There are puzzles like this on the internet too.
2) Play games like 'Cluedo' or 'Guess Who?' to test your powers of deduction and logic.
3) Play 'Twenty Questions' with a friend — it'll help you practise dealing with information.
4) Practise doing sums which use addition and subtraction — doing other Verbal Reasoning questions that use maths will help with this too.
5) Practise putting information into a table — you could ask your friends what pets they have or what shoe size they are and put their answers in a table.

Letter Connections

Letter Connections is another question type that uses the alphabet — you just can't escape it.

Warm-Up Activity

1) This table shows the mirror pairs of all the letters in the alphabet:

A	B	C	D	E	F	G	H	I	J	K	L	M
Z	Y	X	W	V	U	T	S	R	Q	P	O	N

2) Make up word pairs to help you remember each mirror pair, e.g. **A**frican **Z**ebras, **B**rown **Y**ak, **C**lunky **X**ylophone.

3) Learn all 13 pairs and test yourself until you know them all off by heart.

11+ Example Question

Here's an example of the sort of question you might get in the test:

> **Q** Find the pair of letters that completes the sentence in the most sensible way. Use the alphabet to help you.
>
> A B C D E F G H I J K L M N O P Q R S T U V W X Y Z
>
> **GD** is to **JE** as **SB** is to (____).

- There is a connection between the first two letter pairs — you need to work out what this connection is and then apply it to the second pair to find the missing letters.

Method 1 — Count along the alphabet

1) Check to make sure that there aren't any mirror pairs — there aren't any in this example.

2) Next you need to count along the alphabet to see how the first letter in the first pair is connected to the first letter in the second pair.

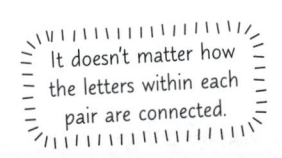

It doesn't matter how the letters within each pair are connected.

GD is to **JE** as **SB** is to (**V**___)

These letters are connected by moving forward 3 places.

Use the connection between the first letters to find the first missing letter.

3) The second letter in the first pair is connected to the second letter in the second pair.

These letters are connected by moving forward 1 place.

Use the connection between the second letters to find the second missing letter.

The letters don't have to move in the same way — they can be completely independent.

GD is to **JE** as **SB** is to (**VC**)

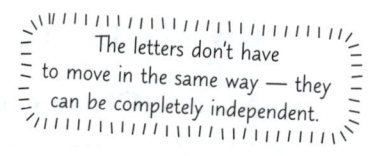

Section Five — Logic and Coding

Check for **Mirror Pairs First**

Q Find the pair of letters that completes the sentence in the most sensible way. Use the alphabet to help you.

A B C D E F G H I J K L M N O P Q R S T U V W X Y Z

ZU is to **FA** as **XS** is to (___).

Method 2 — Use mirror pairs

1) Check the question for mirror pairs. At first glance it may not look like there are any, but on closer inspection...

    Mirror pairs won't always be reversed, so watch out for different mirror pair patterns.

    AZ is a mirror pair, but it's been reversed.

    ZU is to **FA** as **XS** is to (___).

    FU is also a mirror pair and it's been reversed too.

2) The answer will use mirror pairs in the same way as the first pair of letters. The letters in the second pair are **XS**, so find their mirror pairs.

A	B	C	D	E	F	G	H	I	J	K	L	M
Z	Y	X	W	V	U	T	S	R	Q	P	O	N

3) The matching letters are 'C' and 'H'. Now you have to put these letters in the same order as the first pair of letters.

    It's important that you can spot mirror pairs — if you treat a mirror pair like a standard pair of letters then you'll get the wrong answer.

4) So the answer is: ➡ **ZU** is to **FA** as **XS** is to (**HC**).

Practice Questions

Find the pair of letters that completes the sentence in the most sensible way.

1) **DW** is to **FU** as **IR** is to (___).

2) **PF** is to **TB** as **VC** is to (___).

3) **NG** is to **ON** as **SE** is to (___).

4) **BE** is to **YV** as **HK** is to (___).

Section Five — Logic and Coding

Letter-Word Codes

Accurate counting is the key to answering Letter-Word Codes questions.

Warm-Up Activity

Use the code to reveal the punch lines of the jokes below.

E	F	G	H	I	J	K	L	M	N	O	P	Q	R	S	T	U	V	W	X	Y	Z	A	B	C	D
A	B	C	D	E	F	G	H	I	J	K	L	M	N	O	P	Q	R	S	T	U	V	W	X	Y	Z

What do you call an ant who won't go to school? __ __ __ __ __ __ __
                                                                              E   X V Y E R X

What type of tree can grow fingers? __ __ __ __ __ __ __ __ __
                                       E   T E P Q   X V I I

11+ Example Question

Here's an example of the sort of question you might get in the real thing:

> **Key Question**
>
> **Q** **Each question uses a different code.**
> **Use the alphabet to help you work out the answer.**
>
> A B C D E F G H I J K L M N O P Q R S T U V W X Y Z
>
> If the code for **TIN** is **VKP**, what is the code for **MOP**? _____

- You need to work out how to get from the first word to its code, then use the rule to find the code for the second word.
- To find the code, each letter moves 2 places along the alphabet, so the answer is OQR.

The Letters can move in Patterns

1) Within a word each letter can move a different number of places and in a different direction.
2) The jumps between the letters and their codes will form a pattern, e.g. the jumps could increase by one with each letter, or could alternate between two numbers.

> **Continuing the connection**
>
> If the code for **BACK** is **CDDN**, what is the code for **FRUIT**? _____
>
> 1) The second word code can be longer than the first one. In the example above, **BACK** is four letters long whereas **FRUIT** is five letters long.
> 2) To get from the word to the code the letters move forward one place, then forward three places alternately. You can assume the pattern continues for the extra letter, so the fifth letter will move forward one place. This means the answer is GUVLU.

Section Five — Logic and Coding

If you're looking for a **Word**, count from the **Code** to the **Word**

Q Each question uses a different code.
Use the alphabet to help you work out the answer.

A B C D E F G H I J K L M N O P Q R S T U V W X Y Z

If the code for **TUBE** is **SQAA**, what is **AQMG** the code for? _____

Method 1 — Count along the alphabet line

1) Have a look at the question and check for mirror pairs — there aren't any in this example.

2) Work out if you're looking for a word or a code — here, you've been given a code (AQMG), so you're looking for a word.

   If you're looking for a code, you need to work out how to get from the word to the code in the first pair.

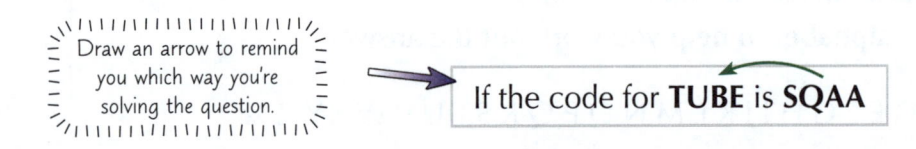

3) When you're looking for a word, look at how you get from the code to the word in the first pair of words.

   Draw an arrow to remind you which way you're solving the question.

   If the code for **TUBE** is **SQAA**

4) Count from each letter of the code to the matching letter of the word.

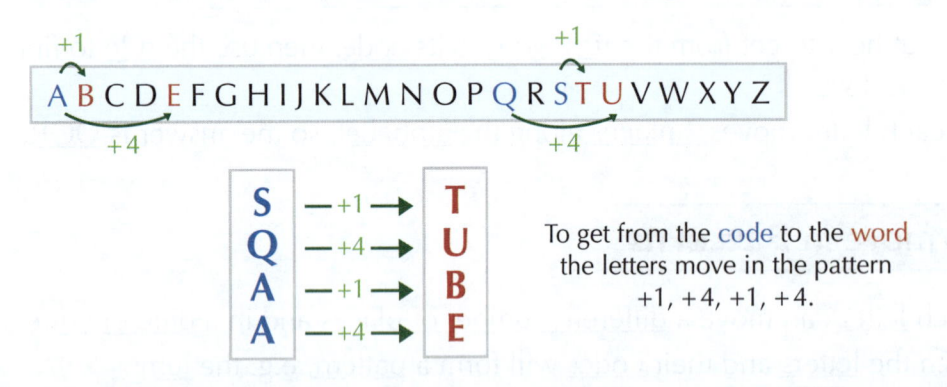

   +1   +1
   A B C D E F G H I J K L M N O P Q R S T U V W X Y Z
   +4   +4

   S —+1→ T
   Q —+4→ U   To get from the code to the word
   A —+1→ B   the letters move in the pattern
   A —+4→ E   +1, +4, +1, +4.

5) Once you know the connection between the word and the code, you can find the missing word.

   A —+1→ B
   Q —+4→ U   To get from the code to the
   M —+1→ N   word move the letters
   G —+4→ K   in the same pattern.

6) The missing word is BUNK.

Tips and Tricks for Letter-Word Codes questions

If you're sitting a multiple-choice test, you might only need to work out the first few letters to find the right answer. If you have time at the end of the test, go back and check your answer.

Section Five — Logic and Coding

Some questions use **Mirror Codes**

Key Question

Q If the code for **STORM** is **HGLIN**, what is **GLDVI** the code for? _____

Method 2 — Check for mirror pairs

1) <u>Mirror pairs</u> can also pop up in Letter-Word Code questions. Here's a <u>reminder</u> of the mirror pairs:

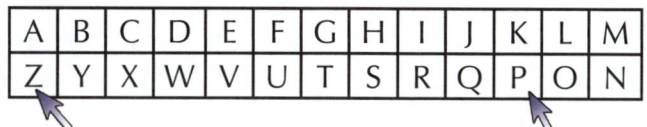

A	B	C	D	E	F	G	H	I	J	K	L	M
Z	Y	X	W	V	U	T	S	R	Q	P	O	N

In questions that use mirror pairs the same letters always code for each other.

Each column is a mirror pair, e.g. A and Z or K and P.

2) Look at the <u>first letters</u> of the <u>word</u> and the <u>code</u> you are given to see if they are a <u>mirror pair</u>.

S → H   S and H are a mirror pair.   H / S
T   G
O   L
R   I
M   N

3) The first letters could be a <u>mirror pair</u> by <u>chance</u> — look at the next <u>two pairs</u> to <u>double check</u>.

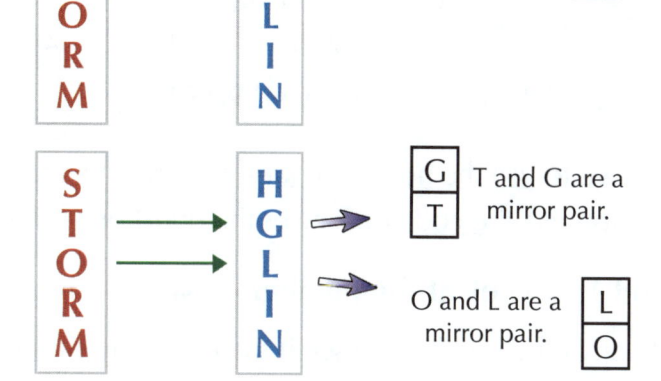

S   H   G / T   T and G are a mirror pair.
T → G
O → L   L / O   O and L are a mirror pair.
R   I
M   N

4) Now that you're <u>sure</u> the question uses a <u>mirror code</u>, use <u>mirror pairs</u> to find the missing word.

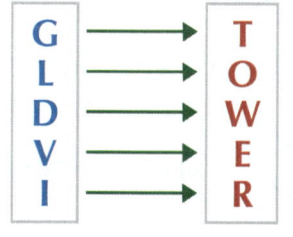

5) The answer is <u>TOWER</u>.

G → T
L → O
D → W
V → E
I → R

If you're looking for a word and your answer doesn't make sense, double check your working.

Practice Questions

Each question uses a different code.
Use the alphabet at the top of the page to help you to answer each question.

1) If the code for **BED** is **GJI**, what is the code for **FIG**? _____
2) If the code for **DARK** is **WZIP**, what is **MRTSG** the code for? _____
3) If the code for **SNOOP** is **VKRLS**, what is **OLBXO** the code for? _____
4) If the code for **HUNT** is **JXRY**, what is the code for **BRING**? _____

Section Five — Logic and Coding

Number-Word Codes

These questions come up a lot, so make sure you know how to answer them.

Warm-Up Activity

1) Make up your own number code for the alphabet — each letter should have a different number.
2) Write a note to a friend using your number code, then ask them to decode it and reply to you in code.

Don't forget to give your friend a copy of the code too, or they won't be able to read your note.

11+ Example Question

Here's an example question for you to take a look at:

Key Question

Q The number codes for three of these four words are listed in a random order. Work out the code to answer the question.

| WEAK   TAKE   PEAT   KEPT |
| 3265   5612   4261 |

Find the code for the word **WEPT**. _____

Usually these questions come in blocks of three.

- You have to use the number codes you are given to work out which number stands for which letter.
- Then you use the code to answer the question — it might be to find a code or a word.

Method 1 — Look at the numbers first

1) Look at the numbers to see if there are any similar patterns.

   (3265)   5612   (4261) ← Both these codes have '26' in the middle.

2) Find the two words that have same two letters in the middle.

   (WEAK)   TAKE   (PEAT)   KEPT → WEAK and PEAT are the only two words that have the same two letters in the middle, so 2 = E and 6 = A.

3) Look at the third number, 5612.

   5 6 1 2 → You know that 2 = E and 6 = A, so you can write these letters below the code. The only word which fits this code is **TAKE**. → 5 6 1 2
   ? A ? E   T A K E

4) Go back to the first two codes and fill in any other letters that you can. You know that 5 = T and 1 = K, so 3265 must code for **PEAT**, and 4261 must code for **WEAK**.

   3 2 6 5   4 2 6 1
   P E A T   W E A K

5) Now you know the number for each letter, you can work out the code for **WEPT**, 4235.

Section Five — Logic and Coding

Compare the Letters in all the words

Key Question

> BELT   DUEL   LUTE   TUBE
> 6415   1526   3452
>
> Find the word that has the number code **1245**. _____

Method 2 — Look for letters in the same position in different words

1) Look at the number codes to see if there are any patterns.

2) None of the number codes end with the same number, so the code for LUTE or TUBE must be missing. Look for other letters that are in the same position in different words.

> BELT   D(U)EL   L(U)TE   T(U)BE → Three of the words have U as a second letter.

3) Look at the number codes. 4 is the second number in two of them, so 4 must be the code for U.

4) BELT is the only word that doesn't have U as its second letter, so the number code that has a different second number must be the code for BELT.

> 6 4 1 5   1 5 2 6   3 4 5 2
> ? U ? ?   B E L T   ? U ? ?

5) Now you can use the code for BELT to crack the remaining codes and answer the question.

> The code that starts with 6 must be the word starting with T. → 6 4 1 5   T U B E
>
> The last code left ends in 2, so this must be the code for the only word ending in L. → 3 4 5 2   D U E L

6) So, the answer is BLUE. → 1 2 4 5   B L U E

Practice Questions

LONE   RENT   NOTE   TOOL
1432   6412   5213

1) Find the code for the word **TOOL**. _____

2) Find the code for the word **TORN**. _____

3) Find the word that has the number code **5466**. _____

Section Five — Logic and Coding

Explore the Facts

This is the first of the logic questions — you'll really need your thinking cap on for these.

Warm-Up Activity

Below is some information about a group of children and their hobbies. Draw a table to show the information. Put the children's names down the side and the hobbies across the top.

- Catherine plays tennis and squash, and goes swimming.
- Amol plays cricket and likes computer games.
- Jonathan plays the trumpet and plays tennis.
- Nina likes knitting and computer games.

11+ Example Question

Take a look at this 11+ sample question:

> **Q Read the information carefully, then use it to answer the question that follows.**
> Gita, Heung, Joseph, Polly and Mark go to an outdoor activity centre.
> Gita, Polly and Heung go rafting. Joseph and Heung go caving.
> Everyone except Gita goes rock climbing. Only Mark goes on the zipwire. Polly does 3 activities.
>
> Who does the **fewest** activities? _____

- You need to read all the information you are given and then use it to answer the question.
- The answer is Gita — when you work through the statements you see she only goes rafting.

Read the Statements carefully

Some phrases can catch you out

In these questions you can't always just count who does what — look out for phrases like these:

- 'All the children...'
- 'All the boys...'
- 'Everyone except...'
- 'Kieran did not...'
- 'The only one who...'

The question could ask you to look for the person who does the most or the fewest things. Make sure you read each sentence carefully so you know what each person is or isn't doing.

Section Five — Logic and Coding

Write the Information down

> **Q** Molly, Ceana, Matt, Dee and Steven are talking about their favourite animals. Molly and Matt like pigs. Matt likes cows. Ceana and Steven like horses. Everyone except Dee likes cows. Dee and Steven like sheep and goats.
>
> Who likes the **most** animals? _____

Method — Make a table

1) Read the question carefully — you need to work out who likes the most animals.

2) Cross out any repeated information so you don't count it twice.

> ~~Matt likes cows.~~ Ceana and Steven like horses. Everyone except Dee likes cows.

3) Read the statements and then put the information into a quick tally chart. Just write the initials — it's quicker than writing whole names.

   If two names have the same initial write the second letter too.

4) Read through each sentence and put a mark next to each initial for the animals they like.

   Initials of people:
   - Mo | ||
   - C | ||
   - Ma | ||
   - D | ||
   - S | ||||

5) Read off the table to answer the question. You're looking for the person who likes the most animals — so that's the person who has the most marks next to their initial.

6) The answer is Steven. *The table doesn't have to be neat as long as the information is clear.*

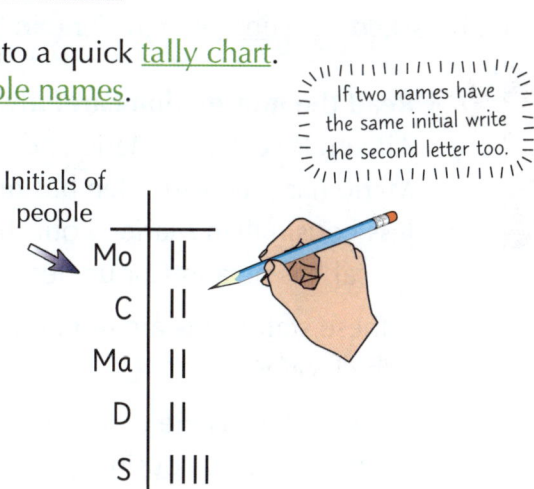

Tips and Tricks for Explore the Facts questions

Remember these questions are only worth one mark each — in the test, make a note of where in the paper they are, then come back to them at the end if you have time.

Practice Questions

Read the information carefully, then use it to answer the question that follows.

Glen, Ali, Kim, Marta and Luca are looking out of the windows of the school bus. Glen and Marta see a pedestrian and a cat. Kim, Ali and Luca see a yellow car. Marta and Ali see a tractor. Everyone except Kim sees a cyclist.

Who sees the **most** different things? _____

Section Five — Logic and Coding

Solve the Riddle

There's lots of information in these questions, so make sure you read each sentence carefully.

Warm-Up Activity

Have a go at answering these riddles.

1) If you are in a race and you overtake the person in second place, what place are you in?

2) A grandfather, two fathers and two sons are competing in an archery contest. They each shoot one arrow. Only three arrows are fired. Why?

3) A farmer has 17 sheep and all but 9 die in a storm. How many are left?

11+ Example Question

You'll be asked questions like this one in the test:

> **Q** **Read the information carefully, then use it to answer the question that follows.**
> Aileen, Pascal, Jen, Marie and Louis are talking about their cousins. Marie has 3 cousins. Jen has more cousins than Louis. Aileen has one less cousin than Marie. Louis has twice the number of cousins Aileen has. Pascal has no aunts or uncles.
>
> If these statements are true, only one of the sentences below **cannot** be true. Which one?
>
>   A Aileen is the oldest of her cousins.
>   B Jen has 5 cousins.
>   C Pascal has the fewest cousins.
>   D Louis has 6 cousins.
>   E Aileen is Jen's cousin.

Sometimes you have to look for the statement that cannot be true and sometimes for the one that must be true.

- Only one option is definitely not true. You need to use the information to work out which one.
- The answer is D. Louis has twice the number of cousins Aileen has, and Aileen has one less cousin than Marie. Marie has 3 cousins, so Louis must have 4 cousins, not 6.

There are different Types of Solve the Riddle questions

1) Solve the Riddle questions will often expect you to put information in order. You might have to order things by time or date, or from oldest to youngest, fastest to slowest, etc.

2) You might not be able to put all the information in order, but you'll always be given enough to answer the question.

3) For some questions you have to use simple maths, e.g. working out people's scores in a game.

These questions are also only worth 1 mark — skip them and come back to them at the end if you have time.

Section Five — Logic and Coding

73

Rule out the Options that are definitely Wrong

Key Question

Q Donald, Ola, Sascha, Sarah and Ravi are playing a word game. Donald scores 96. Ravi wins. Sascha scores 8 more than Donald. Ola scores 30 less than Sascha. Sarah scores 78.

If these statements are true, only one of the sentences below **must** be true. Which one?

- A Ravi scores 110.
- B Ola comes last.
- C Sascha scores less than Sarah.
- D Sarah scores 3 more than Ola.
- E Ola has never played before.

Method 1 — Look for definite facts first

1) Look at the 5 options. The correct answer will be directly related to the information in the question — scan the options to see if any are unrelated.

~~E Ola has never played before.~~ ← You aren't told who has played before so you can ignore this one.

2) To decide between the other options you'll have to do some maths to work out what each person scored. First find any statements that tell you exactly what someone scored.

Donald scores 96.   Sarah scores 78.

3) Look at the other statements and use the information to work out each person's score.

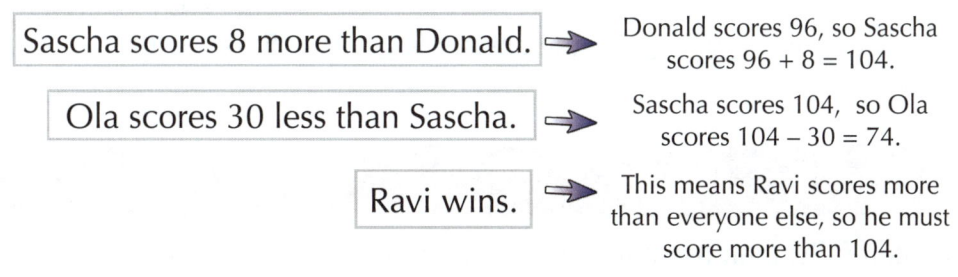

Sascha scores 8 more than Donald. ⇒ Donald scores 96, so Sascha scores 96 + 8 = 104.

Ola scores 30 less than Sascha. ⇒ Sascha scores 104, so Ola scores 104 − 30 = 74.

Ravi wins. ⇒ This means Ravi scores more than everyone else, so he must score more than 104.

4) Now you know everyone's scores, write them as a list and then use the information to choose which statement is true.

Ignore any options that could be true — you're looking for the one that must be true.

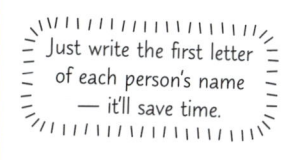

Just write the first letter of each person's name — it'll save time.

R — 104+
Sas — 104
D — 96
Sar — 78
O — 74

⇒
- A Ravi scores 110. **?**
- B Ola comes last. ✓
- C Sascha scores less than Sarah. ✗
- D Sarah scores 3 more than Ola. ✗
- ~~E Ola has never played before.~~

5) The only statement that must be true is B.

Section Five — Logic and Coding

Think about how the Statements Fit Together

Q **Read the information carefully, then use it to answer the question that follows.**
Caitlyn, Stuart, Luke, Mandy and Polly are going to the cinema.
Luke arrives before Caitlyn and Mandy. Polly arrives second.
The third person to arrive is a boy.

If these statements are true, only one of the sentences below **cannot** be true. Which one?

    A Stuart arrives first.
    B Polly arrives before Luke.
    C Mandy arrives before Polly.
    D Caitlyn and Mandy arrive together.
    E Caitlyn arrives after Polly.

Method 2 — Look at each statement one by one

1) Read the statements. You need to work out the order in which everyone arrived.

2) You know Polly arrives second. Use the other statements to work out when the others arrive.

> The third person to arrive is a boy. ⇒ Only Luke or Stuart can arrive third.

> Luke arrives before Caitlyn and Mandy. ⇒ Luke must arrive first or third, so Caitlyn and Mandy must arrive fourth and fifth. If the two girls arrive fourth and fifth, Stuart can only arrive first or third.

3) Scribble down the order they could arrive.

    1st — L / S
    2nd — P
    3rd — L / S
    4th — C / M
    5th — C / M

4) Use your list to choose the correct answer. Here you're looking for the only one that cannot be true.

5) You know Mandy must arrive after Polly, so the answer is C.

Practice Questions

Read the information carefully, then use it to answer the question that follows.
Ellie, Mike, Nathan, Zach and Li are competing in a sack race on sports day.
Mike comes fourth. Zach isn't last. Ellie doesn't win. Li beats Zach. Nathan beats Li.

If these statements are true, only one of the sentences below **cannot** be true. Which one?

    A Ellie comes last.
    B Zach beats Mike.
    C Ellie falls over.
    D Nathan wins.
    E Li comes third.

Word Grids

These are a bit like doing a jigsaw puzzle — but with words instead of pictures.

Warm-Up Activity

Fit these words into the crossword.

ACROSS:
king
gadget
nice
mortar
escape

DOWN:
gong
danger
black
crate

Some letters have been put in to start you off.

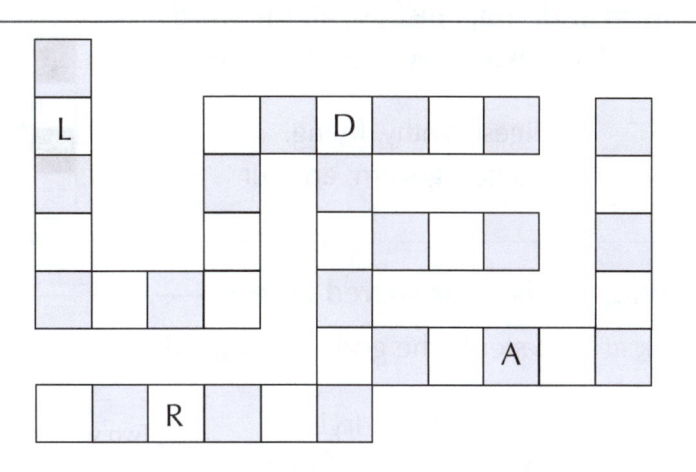

11+ Example Question

Take a look at this 11+ sample question:

Q Use the words to fill in the blanks in the word grid. You must use all the words. One letter has been filled in for you.

puffin, coward, picnic, nagged, fellow

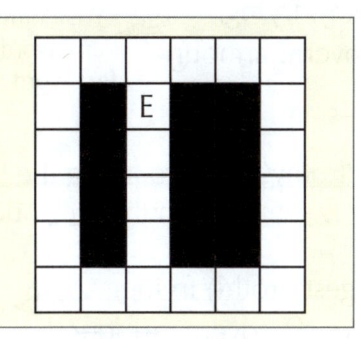

Method 1 — Use the letter you're given

Words go from left to right or top to bottom.

1) Look at the letter in the grid. Count along the grid to find out what position in the word it is. Here E is the second letter in the word.

2) Look at the possible words to see which one has E as its second letter.

puffin, coward, picnic, nagged, f(e)llow

'fellow' is the only word that fits.

3) Now you have clues for two of the other words in the grid — one has W as the third letter and one has F as the third letter.

'puffin' has F as its third letter, so it must go along the top.

pu(f)fin, co(w)ard, picnic, nagged, fellow

'coward' has W as its third letter, so it must go along the bottom.

4) Then use the words you've got left to fill in the gaps.

P	U	F	F	I	N
I		E			A
C		L			G
N		L			G
I		O			E
C	O	W	A	R	D

Section Five — Logic and Coding

Think Ahead to solve Harder questions

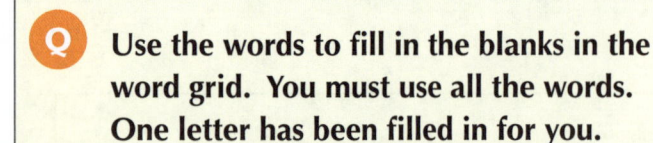

Q Use the words to fill in the blanks in the word grid. You must use all the words. One letter has been filled in for you.

digest, frothy, frying,
agency, govern, armour

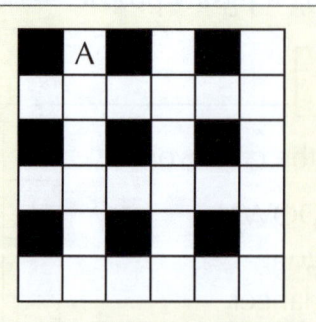

Method 2 — Look for shared letters

1) Look at the letter in the grid — you need a word that starts with A.

   digest, frothy, frying,
   (a)gency, govern, (a)rmour → Two words start with A.

   A is the first letter in a word.

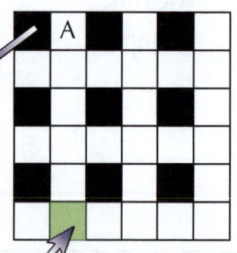

2) The word shares its last letter with the second letter of the word along the bottom. Look at the last letters of 'agency' and 'armour' to see if they are second letters of other words.

   digest, frothy, frying,
   agenc(y) govern, armou(r) → The last letters are Y and R. Y isn't the second letter of any word, but R is, so the first word must be 'armour'. → digest, f(r)othy, f(r)ying, agency, govern, armour

3) Either 'frying' or 'frothy' must go along the bottom — the last letter along the bottom is shared with the word down the right hand side.

   digest, froth(y) frying,
   agenc(y) govern, ~~armour~~ → No words except 'frying' end in g, but 'frothy' shares its last letter with 'agency'.

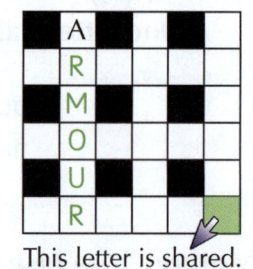

   This letter is shared.

4) 'frothy' must go along the bottom and 'agency' must go down the right hand side.

5) Now you've got a few words in the grid you can fit the rest of the words in.

A			A
R			G
M			E
O			N
U			C
F	R	O	T	H	Y

→

A		D		A
F	R	Y	I	N	G
M		G		E
G	O	V	E	R	N
U		S		C
F	R	O	T	H	Y

Practice Questions

Use the words to fill in the blanks in the word grid. You must use all the words. One letter has been filled in for you.

leeway, nature, circle,
rotten, candle, larvae

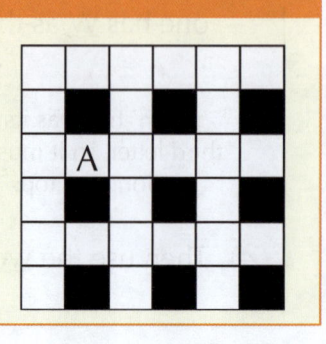

Section Five — Logic and Coding

Glossary

adjective	A word that describes a noun, e.g. 'beautiful morning', 'frosty lawn'.
adverb	A word that describes a verb or an adjective, which often ends with the suffix '-ly', e.g. 'She laughed happily.', 'He ran quickly.'
anagram	When the letters in a word are mixed up, e.g. SWE is an anagram of SEW.
antonym	A word that has the opposite meaning to another, e.g. the antonym of 'good' is 'bad'.
compound word	A word that is made up of two separate words, e.g. 'coast' + 'guard' — 'coastguard'.
consonants	The 21 letters of the alphabet that aren't vowels.
factor	A number you can divide another number by to get a whole number, e.g. 2 is a factor of 6, because 6 ÷ 2 = 3.
Fibonacci sequence	A number sequence where the two previous numbers are added together to give the next number in the sequence, e.g. 1, 2, 3, 5, 8, 13.
homographs	Words that are spelt the same but have different meanings, e.g. 'I want to play.' and 'I saw a play.'
mirror pair	A pair of letters that are an equal distance from the middle of the alphabet in opposite directions, e.g. 'L' and 'O', 'H' and 'S'.
multiple	The number you get when you multiply a whole number by another whole number.
multiple choice	A type of 11+ test that gives you answers to choose from for each question.
noun	A word that names something, e.g. 'Paul', 'cat', 'fear', 'childhood'.
prefix	A string of letters that can be put in front of a word to change its meaning, e.g. 'un-' can be added to 'lock' to make 'unlock'.
prime number	A number that can only be divided by 1 and itself to give a whole number, e.g. 7 can only be divided by 1 and 7.
square number	The number that is made when a number is multiplied by itself, e.g. 3 × 3 = 9, so 9 is a square number.
standard answer	A type of 11+ test that asks you to pick an answer from several options for some questions, and write your own answer for others.
suffix	A string of letters that can be put after a word to change its meaning, e.g. '-er' can be added to the end of 'play' to make 'player'.
synonym	A word with a similar meaning to another word, e.g. 'big' is a synonym of 'huge'.
verb	An action or doing word, e.g. 'run', 'went', 'think'.
vowels	The letters 'a', 'e', 'i', 'o' and 'u'.

Answers

Section One — The Alphabet
Pages 4-5 — Alphabet Positions
Warm-Up Activity
The punch line is 'nice belt'.
Practice Questions
1) a) H
H is at position 8 in the alphabet.
   b) L
L is at position 12 in the alphabet.
   c) P
P is at position 16 in the alphabet.
   d) V
V is at position 22 in the alphabet.
2) a) R
R would be at position 9.
   b) M
M would be at position 14.
   c) G
G would be at position 20.
   d) C
C would be at position 24.
3) a) 14
The middle letter is N, which is at position 14 in the alphabet.
   b) 15
The middle letter is O, which is at position 15 in the alphabet.
   c) 2
The middle letter is B, which is at position 2 in the alphabet.
4) T
T would be at position 12.
5) Z
Z would be at position 20.

Pages 6-7 — Identify a Letter From a Clue
Warm-Up Activity
The letters that don't appear in 'supercalifragilisticexpialidocious' are: b, h, j, k, m, n, q, v, w, y and z.
Practice Questions
1) a) O
O is the letter that occurs most often in NOTORIOUS.
   b) R
R is the letter that occurs most often in FEBRUARY.
   c) S
S is the letter that occurs most often in SHIPMENTS.
2) a) L
L is the only letter that occurs twice in SHALLOW.
   b) N
N is the only letter that occurs twice in RESPLENDENT.
   c) F
F is the only letter that occurs twice in HANDCUFFS.
3) E
E is the only letter that occurs twice in DEADEN, once in DANCER, and once in DANDELION.

Pages 8-9 — Alphabetical Order
Warm-Up Activity
The words go in the order: 1 - aardvark; 2 - antelope; 3 - bear; 4 - bison; 5 - chimp; 6 - eagle; 7 - meerkat; 8 - monkey; 9 - rhino; 10 - snake; 11 - tiger; 12 - zebra.
Practice Questions
1) sparse
The words go in the order — 'spaces', 'sparse', 'spears', 'sporty', 'spring'.
2) confront
The words go in the order — 'conference', 'confides', 'confine', 'confront', 'confuse'.
3) vegetable
The words go in the order — 'unflappable', 'vegetable', 'comfortable', 'constable', 'unstable'.
4) deliberate
The words go in the order — 'complicate', 'inmate', 'deliberate', 'irate', 'frustrate'.

Section Two — Making Words
Page 11 — Preparing for the Test
1) **Answers may vary**
Various answers possible, e.g. 'de-', 'ex-', 'mis-', 'post-' and 'pre-'.
2) a) **Answers may vary**
Various answers possible, e.g. 'stroke', 'string', 'strict', 'stripe'.
   b) **No**
There are no words in English which begin with 'blr'.
   c) **Answers may vary**
Various answers possible, e.g. 'shrink', 'shrub', 'shrug', 'shrine'.
   d) **No**
There are no words in English which begin with 'ds'.
3) a) **CRAZY**
The unscrambled word is CRAZY.
   b) **MIXING**
The unscrambled word is MIXING.
   c) **PLACEMENT**
The unscrambled word is PLACEMENT.

Pages 12-13 — Missing Letters
Warm-Up Activity
Various answers possible, e.g. braineareaIatearlyearunseamelt.
Practice Questions
1) a) f
The new words are 'calf' and 'flap'.
   b) y
The new words are 'toy' and 'you'.
   c) e
The new words are 'toe' and 'elf'.
   d) m
The new words are 'slim' and 'mix'.

2) a) g
The new words are 'dog', 'gap', 'plug' and 'gram'.
   b) s
The new words are 'was', 'soon', 'miss' and 'sun'.

Pages 14-15 — Move a Letter
Warm-Up Activity
The secret message is 'champion'.
Practice Questions
1) l
The new words are 'cone' and 'glad'.
2) p
The new words are 'slit' and 'peel'.
3) p
The new words are 'ride' and 'pair'.
4) r
The new words are 'cook' and 'crow'.
5) e
The new words are 'clan' and 'cape'.
6) w
The new words are 'heat' and 'swell'.

Pages 16-17 — Hidden Word
Warm-Up Activity
Various answers possible, e.g. took — too kind; earn — hear nothing; leap — male ape; hand — orphan dogs; ball — global light; chin — catch ink.
Practice Questions
1) peat
The word is hidden across the words 'turnip eaten'.
2) cake
The word is hidden across the words 'Rebecca keeps'.
3) sofa
The word is hidden across the words 'also farms'.
4) idol
The word is hidden across the words 'placid old'.
5) joke
The word is hidden across the words 'banjo keeps'.
6) inch
The word is hidden across the words 'in cheese'.

Pages 18-19 — Find the Missing Word
Warm-Up Activity
Various answers possible, but can include any three-letter word in a dictionary starting with the letter p, s, a, t or m.
Practice Questions
1) ROW
The complete word is FROWNED.
2) KIT
The complete word is KITTENS.
3) IMP
The complete word is GLIMPSED.

Pages 20-21 — Use a Rule to Make a Word
Warm-Up Activity
The matching pairs are: grin and ring; peal and pale; deal and lead; ship and hips; balm and lamb; ails and sail.
Practice Questions
1) nib
Take letter 3 from the first word, followed by letters 2 and 3 from the second word.
2) asp
Take letter 3 from the second word, followed by letters 1 and 2 from the first word.
3) seat
Take letter 1 from the second word, followed by letter 2 from the first word, then letter 3 from the second word, then letter 4 from the first word.
4) pail
Take letter 3 from the second word, followed by letter 2 from the first word, then letter 2 from the second word, then letter 4 from the first word.

Pages 22-23 — Compound Words
Warm-Up Activity
Various answers possible, but can include any compound word in a dictionary containing the words down, house, bird, in or night — such as 'houseboat', 'bluebird', 'inside' 'nightmare' and 'downstairs'.
Practice Questions
1) rotten
'rotten' is the only correctly spelled word that can be made.
2) beware
'beware' is the only correctly spelled word that can be made.
3) dragon
'dragon' is the only correctly spelled word that can be made.
4) clothe
'clothe' is the only correctly spelled word that can be made.

Pages 24-25 — Complete a Word Pair
Warm-Up Activity
Various answers possible, e.g. super, in, dent, ten, tend, pert, teen, tin, dine, stun, sun.
Practice Questions
1) able
Remove letters 1 and 6, leaving the remaining letters in the order 2, 3, 4, 5.
2) oat
Rearrange letters 2, 3, 5 in the order 5, 2, 3.
3) sat
Rearrange letters 2, 3, 6 in the order 6, 2, 3.
4) rat
Rearrange letters 2, 3, 7 in the order 7, 2, 3.

Pages 26-27 — Anagram in a Sentence
Warm-Up Activity
The words fit together in the following way:

```
 ¹O W ²L       ³M
     E     ²E V E R ⁴Y
 ¹A   A     N         O
 R   ³V A L U E       U
 ⁴M I N I             N
 Y   N               G
     ⁵G R I N
```

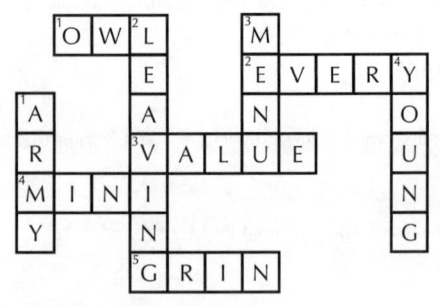

Practice Questions
1) NEPHEWS
NEPHEWS is the only correctly spelled word that fits the sentence.
2) CLOUDY
CLOUDY is the only correctly spelled word that fits the sentence.
3) LASAGNE
LASAGNE is the only correctly spelled word that fits the sentence.
4) CAREFULLY
CAREFULLY is the only correctly spelled word that fits the sentence.
5) SHINGLE
SHINGLE is the only correctly spelled word that fits the sentence.

Page 28 — Word Ladders
Warm-Up Activity
Various answers possible, e.g. team, seam, seal, sell, fell, fall, fail, mail.
Practice Questions
1) (SLED) (FLED)
The ladder is — SPED (SLED) (FLED) FLEA.
2) (BASE) (BASS)
The ladder is — CASE (BASE) (BASS) BOSS.

Section Three — Word Meanings
Page 30 — Preparing for the Test
1 a) verb
'sang' is a verb because it is a doing word.
b) noun
'honesty' is an abstract noun because you can't touch, taste, smell, feel or hear it.
c) adjective
'nosy' is an adjective because it can be used to describe a noun.
d) verb
'tighten' is a verb because it is a doing word.
e) adjective
'cryptic' is an adjective because it can be used to describe a noun.
f) verb & noun
'play' is a verb because it is a doing word. It's also a noun because it is the name of an object or thing.
g) adverb
'vacantly' is an adverb because it describes a verb.

2 a) noun
'truth' is an abstract noun that means 'the reality of a matter'.
b) adjective
'cantankerous' is an adjective that means 'grumpy' or 'disagreeable'.
c) adjective
'wrathfully' is an adverb that means 'angrily'.
d) noun
'bemusement' is a noun that means 'confusion'.

Pages 31-33 — Closest Meaning
Warm-Up Activity
The words fit together in the following way:

```
 ¹H U G E           ³W
 A                   I
 ²P R E T T Y ²N E W
 P           ⁴E N D
 Y           L     Y
     ⁵P A L
```

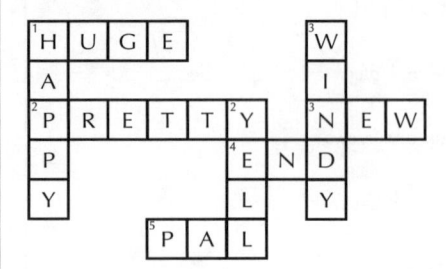

Practice Questions
1) afraid   terrified
Both of these mean 'to be very scared'.
2) trail   track
Both of these mean 'a path' or 'to follow something'.
3) smiled   beamed
Both of these mean 'to grin broadly'.

Pages 34-36 — Opposite Meaning
Warm-Up Activity
Various answers possible, but can include any words with opposite meanings, e.g. happy — sad; poor — rich; serious — jokey; dainty — hefty.
Practice Questions
1) absent   present
'absent' means 'away', whereas 'present' means 'here'.
2) accuse   defend
'accuse' means 'to blame someone', whereas 'defend' means 'to keep someone safe' or 'to argue someone's case'.
3) abolish   establish
'abolish' means 'to end something', whereas 'establish' means 'to start something'.

Pages 37-39 — Multiple Meanings
Warm-Up Activity
Various answers possible, e.g. rich — 'wealthy' or 'creamy or heavy food'. Ruler — 'a straight measuring device' or 'the leader of a group of people.' Match — 'a piece of wood you strike to create fire' or 'a sporting competition'. Fly — 'a winged insect' or 'to move through the air'. Row — 'an argument' or 'to paddle a boat'.
Practice Questions
1) talk
'talk' can mean 'a presentation' or 'to converse'.
2) run
'run' can mean 'to be in charge' or 'to move quickly'.
3) book
'book' can mean 'to arrange something' or 'something you read'.

Answers

Pages 40-41 — Odd Ones Out

Warm-Up Activity

Various answers possible. Suggestions for 'Capital cities' may include: London, Edinburgh, Cardiff, Paris, Berlin, Madrid.

Practice Questions

1) **calm   peaceful**
The other three all mean 'boring'.
2) **poem   novel**
The other three are non-fiction texts.
3) **slumbering   dormant**
The other three all mean 'to feel tired'.

Pages 42-44 — Word Connections

Warm-Up Activity

Various answers possible, e.g. a car has wheels, wheels are also found on a bicycle, when you ride a bicycle you wear a helmet, helmets are worn for safety, safety is part of a fireman's job, firemen use hoses.
Answers for chain 2 may include: dogs chew bones, bones make up skeletons, skeletons can be scary, some people are scared of spiders, spiders spin webs, the world wide web is another name for the internet.

Practice Questions

1) **shell   coat**
They are the outer coverings of lobsters and dogs.
2) **scissors   telescope**
They are the objects that cut and magnify.
3) **unlucky   bald**
They are the opposites of 'fortunate' and 'hairy'.

Pages 45-46 — Reorder Words to Make a Sentence

Warm-Up Activity

Various answers possible, e.g. The farmer milked his cows in the barn. I ate my pizza while I read my book. Josephine has red hair and blue eyes.

Practice Questions

1) **Quickly   take**
The sentence is — 'Take the footpath if you want to get there quickly'.
2) **Fluffy   Nan**
The sentence is — 'My Nan has a pet Beagle called Fluffy'.
3) **bolts   robot**
The sentence is — 'The robot had silver bolts and blue wires'.
4) **week   a**
The sentence is — 'It's my birthday a week today'.

Section Four — Maths and Sequences

Pages 49-50 — Complete the Sum

Warm-Up Activity

The answers to the sums are:

			6	×	3	+	2	=	20
			÷		×				×
20			3		8	÷	4	=	2
−			=		+				=
16	−	14	=	2	8				40
=					=				
4	×	5	+	12	=	32			

Practice Questions

1) **20**
11 × 4 = 44, 44 = 24 + 20
2) **7**
30 − 4 = 26, 26 = 19 + 7
3) **4**
54 ÷ 9 = 6, 6 = 2 + 4
4) **7**
25 + 10 = 35, 35 = 5 × 7
5) **9**
3 × 7 + 4 = 25, 25 = 16 + 9
6) **4**
30 ÷ 6 − 2 = 3 , 3 = 12 ÷ 4
7) **18**
15 × 3 ÷ 5 = 9, 9 = 27 − 18
8) **6**
18 ÷ 3 × 2 + 4 = 16, 16 = 10 + 6

Pages 51-53 — Letter Sequences

1) **UZ**
Both letters move forward 2 letters each time.
2) **EY**
The first letter moves forward 5 letters each time. The second letter moves back 4 letters each time.
3) **KR**
The first letter moves forward 1 letter, then forward 3 letters alternately. The second letter moves forward 4 letters each time.
4) **IS**
The first letter moves in the sequence +1, 0, -1, -2, -3. The second letter moves forward two letters, then four letters alternately.

Answers

Pages 54-56 — Number Sequences

Warm-Up Activity

7 times table: 21, 28, 35, 49, 56, 84.
3 times table: 12, 15, 18, 21, 84.
5 times table: 15, 20, 35, 40.

Practice Questions

1) 34
The numbers follow the sequence -4, -5, -4, -5.
2) 43
Add even numbers in ascending order: +4, +6, +8, +10.
3) 11
Subtract prime numbers in descending order: -11, -7, -5, -3.
4) 3
Divide each number by 3 each time.

Pages 57-59 — Related Numbers

Warm-Up Activity

Various answers possible, e.g.
5 × 11 − 3 = 52
9 ÷ 3 × 10 + 13 + 2 = 45
5 × 2 × 9 + 3 = 93
10 ÷ 2 × 9 − 9 = 36

Practice Questions

1) 38
Add the two outer numbers.
2) 31
Multiply the two outer numbers and then subtract 1.
3) 8
Divide the third number by the first number and double the result.
4) 22
Find the mid-point between the two outer numbers by adding the outer numbers together and dividing the answer by 2.

Pages 60-61 — Letter-Coded Sums

Warm-Up Activity

Various answers possible, e.g.
B × E = 10
C × C + A = 10
D ÷ B × E = 10
D × E ÷ B = 10

Practice Questions

1) E
7 × 4 = 28, E = 28
2) E
11 × 3 − 14 = 19, E = 19
3) D
45 ÷ 9 × 3 = 15, D = 15
4) A
12 × 4 − 17 − 27 = 4, A = 4

Section Five — Logic and Coding

Pages 63-64 — Letter Connections

1) KP
These are mirror pairs. F is two letters forwards from D, so the answer is KP because K is two letters forwards from I, and P is its mirror pair.
2) ZY
The first letter in the pair moves forward 4 letters, the second letter moves back 4 letters.
3) TL
The first letter in the pair moves forward 1 letter, the second letter moves forward 7 letters.
4) SP
These are mirror pairs. B and Y are a mirror pair, as are E and V. The corresponding mirror pairs for H and K are S and P.

Pages 65-67 — Letter-Word Codes

Warm-Up Activity

The punch lines are: 'a truant' and 'a palm tree'.

Practice Questions

1) KNL
To get from the word to the code, move each letter forward 5.
2) NIGHT
To get from the code to the word, find the mirror pair for each letter.
3) LOYAL
To get from the code to the word, move the letters in the sequence -3, +3, -3, +3, -3.
4) DUMSM
To get from the word to the code, move the letters in the sequence +2, +3, +4, +5, +6.

Pages 68-69 — Number-Word Codes

1) 3446
T = 3, O = 4, O = 4, L = 6
2) 3451
T = 3, O = 4, R = 5, N = 1
3) ROLL
R = 5, O = 4, L = 6, L = 6

Pages 70-71 — Explore the Facts

Warm-Up Activity

The table should look something like this:

	Tennis	Squash	Swimming	Cricket	Comp. games	Knitting	Trumpet
Catherine	✓	✓	✓				
Amol				✓	✓		
Nina				✓		✓	
Jonathan	✓						✓

Practice Question

1) Marta
Marta sees a pedestrian, a cat, a tractor and a cyclist.

Answers

Pages 72-74 — Solve the Riddle

Warm-Up Activity

1) Second

If you overtake the person in second place, you are now second and the person in second place is now third.

2) There are only three men.

The grandfather is both a grandfather and a father. His son is both a son and a father.

3) 9

The riddle says that "all but 9 die".

Practice Question

1) E

Nathan beat Li, and Li beat Zach. Zach didn't come last, and he can't have come fourth, so Zach must have come third and Li must have come second.

Pages 75-76 — Word Grids

Warm-Up Activity

The words fit into the grid in the following way:

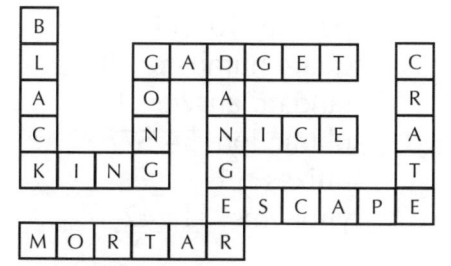

B								
L		G	A	D	G	E	T	
A		O		A				C
C		N		N	I	C	E	R
K	I	N	G					A
			E	S	C	A	P	E
M	O	R	T	A	R			

Practice Question

C	I	R	C	L	E
A	■	O	■	A	■
N	A	T	U	R	E
D	■	T	■	V	■
L	E	E	W	A	Y
E	■	N	■	E	■

This is the only way all the words fit together in the grid.

Index

A
addition 54, 57
adjectives 29
adverbs 29
alphabet 2, 4-9, 48, 51, 63-67
alphabet circle 48
Alphabetical Order 8, 9
Alphabet Positions 4, 5
alternate numbers 55
Anagram in a Sentence 26, 27
antonyms 34, 42

C
Closest Meaning 31-33
coding 62-69
Complete a Word Pair 24, 25
Complete the Sum 49, 50
Compound Words 22, 23

D
division 54-57
drawing tables 62, 70, 71

E
Explore the Facts 70, 71

F
factors 47, 56
Fibonacci sequences 48, 54
Find the Missing Word 18, 19

H
Hidden Word 16, 17
homographs 37

I
Identify a Letter From a Clue 6, 7

L
Letter-Coded Sums 60, 61
Letter Connections 63, 64
Letter Sequences 51-53
Letter-Word Codes 65-67
logic 2, 62, 70-76

M
maths 2, 47-50, 54-61
mental maths 2, 47
mirror codes 63-67
Missing Letters 12, 13
Move a Letter 14, 15
multiple choice 1
Multiple Meanings 37-39
multiples 47, 56
multiplication 54-57

N
nouns 29
Number Sequences 54-56
Number-Word Codes 68, 69

O
Odd Ones Out 40, 41
Opposite Meaning 34-36

P
prefixes 10, 34
preparing for the 11+ 3
prime numbers 48
pronunciation 22

Q
question types 2

R
Related Numbers 57-59
Reorder Words to Make a Sentence 45, 46
riddles 72

S
sequences 48, 51-56
Solve the Riddle 72-74
spelling 10, 11
square numbers 48
standard answer 1
subtraction 54-57
suffixes 11
synonyms 31, 42

T
times tables 2, 47, 50, 60

U
Use a Rule to Make a Word 20, 21

V
verbs 29
vocabulary 2, 29, 40

W
Word Connections 42-44
Word Grids 75, 76
Word Ladders 28
word meanings 2, 29-44
word types 29-36, 41, 44, 46